The Mystic City

ISBN 978-1-7373835-0-5

Beydler Publishing

Printed by Kindle Direct Publishing

First edition June 2021

Front cover

Parade participants get ready to step off as a crowd gathers near Broadway and Main in Jerico in this undated photograph from Dr. Bill Neale's collection. It was probably taken around 1890.

Back cover

A 1903 photo captures the Pickett Block, left, and the Gates Block, both of which were destroyed by fires set by arsonists June 4-5, 1904.

About the title

"Mystic City" was a commonly used synonym for Jerico during its first decade. Like so much about the town's early years, the "why" is a mystery, but it seems an appropriate title for a story about that time, when business boomed and hopes were high.

Acknowledgements

The people deserving most credit for this work are Missouri's country newspaper editors of the late 19th Century. Without their "first draft of history" this book would have been quite impossible.

Dr Bill Neale, whose ancestors include J. B. Carrico Sr. and Charles Whitsitt, was generous with his time, family stories and photographs from his private collection. Others who have shared old Jerico photos with me include Kim Jefferies, Charles Skaggs and Chrisanne Mitchell-Freeborn.

Greg Gackle volunteered his considerable design skills to put together the cover for this book, and Michael Ashcraft cast his eagle eye over the final manuscript, thereby saving me several embarrassments.

The Wednesday Night Pie Guys get a thank you, too, for not kicking me out of the group for providing too-frequent updates on my Jerico research.

Author's note

Jerico Springs' founders left no journals outlining their plans, no diaries taking note of the daily triumphs and disappointments as the town rose from a prairie hillside, no character-revealing bundles of letters.

There is a record nevertheless, buried in long-ago magazines, gazetteers, advertising directories, government reports and - especially – newspapers. Most helpful among those surviving from the 1880-1910 period - on microfilm or digitally - were the *Jerico Springs Optic*, the *Stockton Journal*, the *Cedar County Republican*, the *Nevada Noticer*, the *El Dorado Springs Sun*, the *Sheldon Enterprise*, The *Lamar Missourian*, the *Lamar Democrat*, the *Lockwood Luminary*, the *Greenfield Vedette* and the *Dade County Advocate*.

The record compiled therein shows that while Jerico's founders ultimately failed and are forgotten, the effort they put forth is worthy of at least a short song.

 - jcb, May, 2021

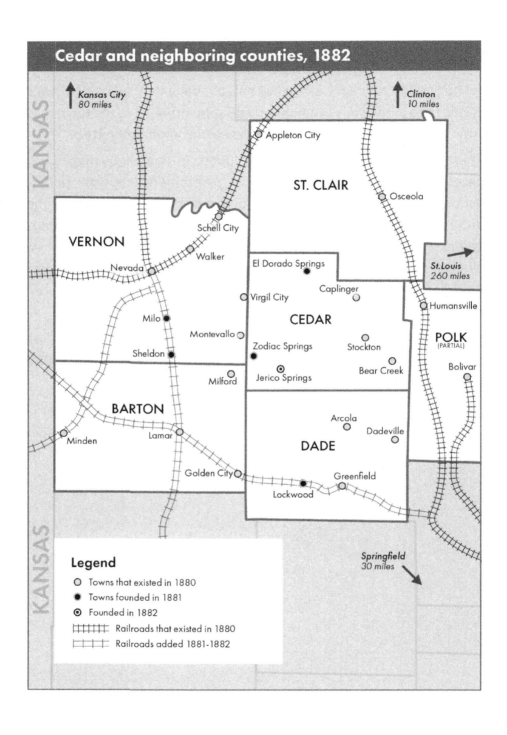

Cedar and neighboring counties, 1882

Kansas City
80 miles

Clinton
10 miles

KANSAS

KANSAS

ST. CLAIR

Appleton City

Osceola

Schell City

VERNON

Walker

Nevada

El Dorado Springs

Caplinger

St.Louis
260 miles

Virgil City

Humansville

CEDAR

Milo

POLK
(PARTIAL)

Montevallo

Zodiac Springs

Stockton

Sheldon

Bolivar

Bear Creek

Milford

Jerico Springs

Arcola

BARTON

Lamar

Dadeville

DADE

Minden

Golden City

Greenfield

Lockwood

Springfield
30 miles

Legend

○ Towns that existed in 1880

● Towns founded in 1881

◉ Founded in 1882

╫╫╫╫ Railroads that existed in 1880

┼┼┼ Railroads added 1881-1882

The Mystic City

A History of Jerico Springs, Missouri

John C. Beydler

Table of Contents

Foreword

Jerico Springs, Mo., population about 230, is a dirt-street town with an over-sized business district filled with empty lots and crumbling buildings. Neatly kept homes provide evidence of life, though every block seems to have at least one lot where a bulldozer is needed.

There's a pleasant park around a spring in the middle of town, which sets on a pair of low hills divided by a small stream in Cedar County, 110 miles south and a little east of Kansas City. It's a pretty place, particularly in Spring and Autumn, and there are a good many nice people living there.

Beyond that, there isn't much - except a story.

1. The gathering

Sometime in the Spring of 1844, Joseph B. Carrico, 26, and his wife, Eleanor, of similar age, left their home in Nelson County in central Kentucky and set out to the West. There is no record of their precise reasons for leaving but their goal is as clear as it was common at the time: new opportunities in a new place.

It's unlikely the two had more than a general sense of where they were going when they undertook what would prove to be a 500-mile journey that most probably led them first overland to Louisville and then down the Ohio River and across the Mississippi into southeast Missouri. From there, they would have gone another 300 miles or so overland to the state's western border region, where there was government land available.

The area into which the Carricos traveled, home to various Native American groups over the ages, had been controlled by the Osage Nation in 1682 when the explorer LaSalle claimed all land drained by the Mississippi River for France. In 1803 France sold its claim to the United States as part of the Louisiana Purchase, and in 1808 the Osage ceded their rights to the U.S. for little more than a token payment.

In the Land Act of 1820, Congress set the conditions for claiming public land that prevailed when Missouri became a state in 1821 and for 40 years thereafter: Minimum purchase was 80 acres, down from the 160 previously required; the price dropped from a minimum $2 an acre to $1.25 an acre, cash on the barrel head. The changes intended to increase the number of people able to afford a move to the frontier.

The first white settlers in what would become Cedar County arrived in 1832, settling as did most early arrivals in the rich land in the Sac River valley. The population was barely out of the dozens when Joe and Eleanor Carrico arrived in 1844.

They passed over the more heavily forested eastern regions of the future county, traveling a final 15 miles or so westward into a rolling prairie cut by small streams running through wooded valleys and dotted with springs. They picked a home site near three small springs clustered around each other toward the bottom of a gently sloping hillside.

The first of the men who would build Jerico was on the scene.

Whether the $1.25 an acre cost for land was too much for him or he was simply unconcerned about securing title in the sparsely populated region, Mr. Carrico went about building a home and family without claiming land, a detail he put off for a decade.

Cedar County was formed in February of 1845, and Mr. Carrico began a life-long commitment to civic life by serving as a Benton Township election judge when Cedar County conducted its first election that year.

Mr. Carrico also took an active part in the new community's religious life. The Cedar Association, an early grouping of Baptist churches in Cedar County, named him an itinerant minister in 1852, according to Goodspeed Publishing Company's 1889 *History of Hickory, Polk, Cedar, Dade, and Barton Counties, Missouri.*

A devout man who was curious and questioning about religion, Mr. Carrico was born a Catholic but switched to Protestantism after learning to read.   At some point, probably in the 1870s, that questioning spirit got him in trouble with the Baptists.

"It came to the attention of the authorities that his preaching did not exactly match the established teachings of the denomination," said Dr. Bill Neale of EL Dorado Springs, Mo., a descendant who still has Mr. Carrico's Bible with its hand-written notes. "An authority was sent from St. Louis, and a debate was held at the Round Prairie Church. It took 3 days, and some present said (Carrico) won. Nevertheless, he was 'churched' and removed as a Baptist minister." He then joined the Christian Church and was later minister at that denomination's Jerico church.

The home site the Carricos chose upon their arrival allowed them a glimpse into the past as small groups of Native Americans occasionally visited the nearby springs. Given Mr. Carrico's personality and wide-ranging curiosity, he is certain to have been friendly with the visitors and interested in their lives. They told him they drank the water from the springs and bathed in it and its mud to find relief for various ailments, though details about which ailments are lost in now-silent oral tradition.

The visits by Native Americans faded away with the 1840s, but the use of the springs for medicinal purposes was taken up by the whites gradually moving into Cedar County and Benton Township. Carrico Springs, as they came to be known, built at least a local reputation for their health benefits, though again there is no early record of exactly what those benefits were said to be.

By 1850, Cedar County had grown to 3,361 people. Benton Township, with its open prairies, remained sparsely populated. That would change rapidly during the 1850s, by the end of which virtually all the government land in Cedar County had been claimed.

Along with more neighbors, the new decade apparently brought a degree of prosperity to the Carricos. In early 1854, he acquired 80 acres immediately east of the future town, the first of several parcels he would file for at the government land office in Springfield during the 1850s.

Later in 1854, when 26-year-old Crafton J. Beydler arrived on foot after a 1,000-mile journey from the Shenandoah Valley in Virginia, Mr. Carrico was able to hire the newcomer to split rails and otherwise assist on the farm. Mr. Beydler, who claimed his own land a mile north of the future town in 1856, would play a minor role in Jerico's civic affairs though his life intertwined closely with that of the town and those of several of its major figures.

In early 1856, Morris W. Mitchell, 29, the second of Jerico's builders to arrive, bought 40 acres southeast of the future town and would soon acquire more. A preacher's son, he was born in Tennessee July 1, 1821 and moved with his parents when he was 15 to Polk County, Missouri, which borders Cedar on the east. An adventurous sort, he joined the Army, fought in the Mexican War and had been to the California goldfields before arriving in Benton Township. He would further tour the battlefields of the Civil War before serving on Jerico's first city council and in banking, mercantile and political life there.

The third of Jerico's founders to arrive was born on the spot. Joseph B. Carrico Jr., the sixth of Joe and Eleanor Carrico's seven children, was born Aug. 26, 1856. Twenty-five years old when Jerico was laid out in 1881-82, he would play a longer and larger role there than his father.

The fourth key figure arrived in 1857 when the Isham Brasher family from Kentucky settled a mile or so west of the future town. Isham's son, Joseph P. Brasher, then seven years old, would serve on Jerico's first city council and play prominent roles in medicine, banking and politics.

As the 1850s wound down, the future in many ways looked bright all around. The basic outline of Missouri's rail system was rapidly filling in, enabling growth that saw the population increase by a half million during the decade. Cedar County's soared by 97 percent, to 6,637, of which 614 lived in Benton Township. An astonishing 48.4 percent of the county population was less than 15 years old, betokening growth to come.

In an ominous reminder that all was not well, the county's slave population also grew rapidly, more than doubling from 82 to 211 during the 1850s. One hundred and eighty-five of them were held in Madison, Linn and Benton townships, along the county's southern border. There were 25 slaves in Benton Township, eight of them held by Morris Mitchell. The township borders Barton and Vernon counties on the west and is barely 30 miles from the Kansas border, a matter of considerable import in the years leading up to 1860.

 Low-key fighting began along the border with the 1854 passage of the Kansas-Nebraska Act, which provided the two territories would decide by a vote of their residents whether they would enter the union as free or slave states. Supporters of both sides poured into Kansas hoping to take part in the vote.

There was soon open fighting between pro- and anti-slavery forces and it quickly spilled into Missouri as anti-slavers raided across the entire length of the border, stealing and freeing slaves and increasingly hauling off whatever else took their fancy. Missourians rode into Kansas to recover the stolen slaves and other property. Increasingly they, too, stole whatever took their fancy. Tit for tat soon reigned. Killing grew common.

The violence hit Cedar County, too. *Campbell's Missouri Gazetteer for 1874* said in its Cedar County section, "During the late Kansas troubles … the hostile parties … met upon its soil." Other incursions into neighboring Vernon and Barton counties by anti-slavery forces out of Kansas helped fan pro-south sentiment among even the majority non-slave holders.

2. *The gathering interrupted*

n the fateful election of 1860, winner Abraham Lincoln got only 4 votes out of 871 cast in Cedar County and just 10.3 percent in Missouri overall. County and state were carried by Stephen Douglas, a slavery-tolerant U. S. senator from Illinois who got about a third of the vote in the four-candidate election. Nationally, Lincoln won with 39 percent of the popular vote.

As the nation divided, Missouri stayed in the union though a government-in-exile represented it in the Confederate Congress as well. The split that sent tens of thousands of Missourians into the armies of both North and South was tragically reflected in Cedar and neighboring counties, where families and neighbors turned on each other. The fighting, primarily by militia units, irregulars and guerrillas, was no less savage for being small scale.

It scarred every town then existing in Cedar and neighboring counties and permanently wiped some off the map. Hamlets called Centerville, about 18 miles northwest of Stockton, and White Hare, about six miles southeast of the future Jerico, were among those destroyed in the fighting and never rebuilt.

Stockton, held by Union supporters, fortified the Cedar County Courthouse and held off one big guerrilla attack there. But Confederate Col. Jo Shelby's force of 1,000 or so men burned the building as he moved north in October of 1863 on his famous raid from Arkansas deep into Central Missouri. Several mills in Cedar County were burned along with "most of the farmhouses in the western part of the county," according to the *Campbell's Missouri Gazetteer*.

Greenfield and Lamar, also county seat towns, were fought over several times, including one fight at Lamar in which the infamous guerrilla William Quantrill led the attackers.

Nevada, the Vernon County seat and effectively the headquarters of the southern-aligned bushwhackers who posed a constant threat to Union-loyal residents of multiple counties, was burned by militia units from Cedar and St. Clair counties May 23, 1863. They torched the business district, along with 75 houses, though residents were given 20 minutes notice before their homes were set afire. Spared was only the jail and a handful of houses known to belong to Union men.

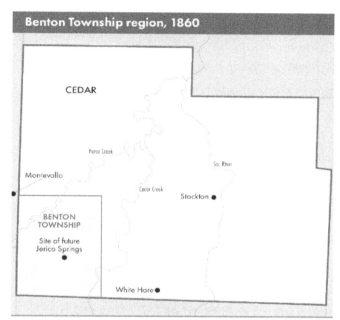

Benton Township region, 1860

CEDAR

Horse Creek

Sac River

Montevallo

Cedar Creek

Stockton ●

BENTON TOWNSHIP

Site of future Jerico Springs ●

White Hare ●

On their way home, the Cedar County men killed seven of a group of guerrillas they surprised near Montevallo, a hamlet on the Vernon-Cedar County line that was a hotbed of bushwhacker activity and which was the scene of several big fights. It was rebuilt after the war about a mile west of its original site.

As the Cedar County militiamen continued on through Benton Township on their way to Stockton, they would have crossed both Horse and Cedar creeks, the rugged bottoms of which were favored hideaways for the bushwhackers. Union forces often searched and fought along the two creeks.

A pair of typical reports from Union officers, one from 1862 and the other from 1864, provide further insight into the nature of the fighting around and in Benton Township:

SPRINGFIELD MO September 11 1862

GENERAL

I have the honor to report that in obedience to your Special Orders No 623 I marched at 8 o clock pm 5th instant (of this month) with ... a total aggregate of 286 men afterward increased by Captain Smith's command numbering 44 men making 330.

At 11 o clock pm 6th instant I marched for the head of Horse Creek with the entire command above reported. Along the whole route I kept out advance and flanking parties. Arrived at Waggoner's head of Horse Creek Barton County at 12 pm 7th instant, found numerous signs of rebel guerrilla parties. For about five hours we were constantly chasing gangs of bushwhackers varying in numbers from 4 to 25. Camped on Horse Creek 8th. Left camp at 4 o clock am. Divided the force and scouted both the Cedar Creek and Horse Creek country thoroughly arriving at Stockton at 6 o clock pm staid until 2 o clock am 9th.

Started south scouring both creeks arriving at Greenfield 5 o clock pm 10th. Left Greenfield 4 o clock am. At Pemberton Mills dismissed all of Enrolled Militia to return to their respective precincts and came to Springfield arriving in camp at 1.30 o clock am 11th making in all a march estimated at 250 miles at least.

During the expedition I know that 11 bushwhackers were killed and several wounded There is a considerable force of guerrillas, say 200 or 250, on the two creeks Horse and Cedar who are scattered over a large area of country in small squads. The extreme density of the growth of brush in the timber makes it impenetrable to a stranger. I would respectfully suggest the only way in which they can be removed viz to send a force there for the purpose of staying until they are exterminated taking provisions upon which to subsist as the country affords nothing.

Very respectfully your obedient servant,

JNO E COLLINS, Major, Eighth Cavalry Missouri State Militia
General TOTTEN Comdg Southwest Division Missouri Springfield
Mo.

The situation was little changed two years later when bushwhackers attacked Melville, (now Dadeville) a hamlet northeast of Greenfield in Dade County, apparently while its defenders were out looking for them.

Report of Capt. Calvin S. Moore, Sixth Missouri State Militia
Cavalry.

HDQRS.,

Greenfield, Mo., June 14, 1864.

GEN.: Melville was attacked this morning about sunrise by about 75 bushwhackers; they succeeded in burning the town and killing several men, mostly citizens. I think there were only a few militia there and I think they were completely surprised. Maj. Morgan, with most of the men there, was on a scout in the Horse Creek country. The rebels came in from a northwest direction; were commanded by Pete Roberts.

C. S. MOORE,

Capt., Cmdg.

Two days later, Capt. Moore, who had promised to mount a quick pursuit, filed this report:

HDQRS. POST,

Greenfield, Mo., June 16, 1864.

GEN.: I have the honor to report that the command that left here on the 14th instant in pursuit of the bushwhackers that burned Melville, Mo., on the 14th instant, formed a junction with a portion of Enrolled Missouri and citizens from Melville and vicinity about 4 o'clock on the same day they left here. Struck the trail of the rebels at 4 o'clock, and followed it until dark, when the rebels scattered. The command then went 15 miles in the direction of Lamar, to try to strike the trail of rebels. Camped on Horse Creek about midnight. Started in pursuit again on the morning of the 15th and came on the rebels in camp about 12 o'clock, 15th. The rebels were selling off at auction to one another the goods they had stolen at Melville before they burned the town. They were taken somewhat by surprise. Our men immediately charged them and routed them, killing 7 rebels and wounding a number more, and capturing almost all the goods they had stolen, together with about 15 horses. Our troops all did well. The rebels scattered. Our men were too much fatigued to pursue them.

A large portion of the captured property was turned over on the spot to the citizens at Melville that claimed them. A portion of it is in the hands of the Enrolled Missouri Militia that participated in the fight. A portion of it my men brought off, consisting of dry goods, &c., which I have taken possession of and will turn over to legal owners upon their identifying the same. Our loss was none killed, 1 or 2 Enrolled Missouri Militia slightly wounded.

C. S. MOORE,

Capt., Cmdg. Post.

Horse Creek flows through the western and northern parts of Benton Township. Cedar Creek runs along its eastern border. Many Benton Township residents fled to escape the violence.

Others were forced out. At some point - probably 1863 - pro-southern forces drove out Joseph Carrico, Crafton Beydler and "many" of their neighbors. Their stock and other property was stolen or destroyed and they were told to get out the county within 24 hours or be killed.

The group fled, at least some of them going all the way to central Illinois, where they waited out the war. Other township residents fled westward into central Kansas. The Cedar County violence also touched Morris Mitchell, who was away at war as a captain in the Confederate Army. His father-in-law, John Lindley, was shot dead while sowing wheat at his farm. Capt. Mitchell, whose unit was among the last Southern forces to give up the fight, returned home after the war to find his own house and outbuildings burned and his fields overtaken by weeds.

He joined other returning soldiers and refugees, including the Carricos and Beydlers, in picking up the pieces and rebuilding their lives.

3 The gathering, resumed

Along with the returning refugees and soldiers, newcomers found their way to Benton Township.

On Feb. 16, 1868, two foot-weary travelers from Virginia's Shenandoah Valley trudged up the road to Crafton Beydler's house. One was his brother, Jacob; the other, James K. Peer. Both were former Confederate soldiers looking for new homes.

Mr. Peer, 23, soon bought a farm but when Jerico was founded 14 years later he was among the first to build there, first a hotel and then a successful mercantile house for which he eventually bought hardware by the carload. He would send as many as 12 wagons at a time to the rail station in Lockwood to haul it the final 20 miles to Jerico.

In 1870, Francis M. Bruster, five years old, arrived when his father bought a farm four miles north of the future town. Too young to play any role when Jerico was planned, he became first a widely admired teacher and after 1896, a lawyer and real estate agent who was among Jerico's most indefatigable boosters.

A man who would have more immediate impact arrived in 1875 when James A. Cogle, 41, bought a farm a mile and a half south of the future town. Born in Indiana in 1834, he was a school teacher in Richwoods, Ark., when the Civil War broke out. He and his new wife, Matilda, moved to St. Louis, where he joined the Union Army in 1861. A lieutenant in an artillery unit at war's end, he left the Army and moved to Stockton, where he farmed and got into politics, being elected to a term as Cedar County clerk as a Republican. He would open Jerico's first store and play a leading role in politics there.

Sometime between 1876 and 1880, Daniel G. Stratton arrived in Cedar County, settled near Stockton and started buying land. A former merchant and farmer in Cambridge, Ill., he was listed on the 1870

Census as "retired person." He was around 50 years old when for reasons unrecorded he picked Cedar County as a place to begin a new career as a land speculator and prospector. Jerico would be his creation.

In late 1880 or early 1881, Charles E. Whitsitt, who lived south of Nevada, bought a farm just west of Carrico Springs. A native of Kentucky, Mr. Whitsitt, in his early 30s, had been in western Missouri since he was 12. Listed as a clerk in a Pleasant Hill furniture store in the 1870 Census, he was by 1880 listed as a farmer just south of Nevada. It's likely Mr. Whitsitt made his move because he and Daniel Stratton had discussed plans for a town and Mr. Whitsitt saw it as a place where his entrepreneurial spirit could find an outlet. In any case, the two men collaborated closely in launching Jerico and their relationship endured until – and even past – Mr. Stratton's death 20 years later.

With Mr. Whitsitt's arrival, the central figures in Jerico's founding and booming early growth were gathered. The eight of them ranged in age from 25 to 63. Except for Mr. Stratton and Mr. Whitsitt, they had lived within five miles of the future town site for years, some for decades. They were nevertheless well-traveled men for the time with considerable experience of the world. They had lived in other places and were on a second or third career. Two had served in county-wide elective offices. Three had fought in the Civil War, two South and one North, and at least two others had been war refugees. They apparently succeeded in putting aside whatever differences had existed in a conflict now 17 years over.

A recap, by order of descending age:

- **Joseph B. Carrico Sr., 63** in 1881 as the town was planned, had traveled from Kentucky to Benton Township 37 years earlier. A farmer, preacher and homespun intellectual who dabbled in politics, he had run for the state legislature in 1878 as a candidate of the Greenback Party, an alliance of farmers and workers favoring loose-money. The owner of more than 400 acres just north of the town site, he was known and respected throughout Cedar County, being in demand as a speaker and lecturer.

- **Morris W. Mitchell, 60,** a Tennessee native, had fought in two wars, been to the California goldfields and served as Cedar County sheriff from 1858-1860 and later as county collector. A farmer with some 400 acres southeast of the town site, he, too, was known and respected throughout Cedar County.

- **Daniel G. Stratton, 53**, the Ohio native like all the others had a farming background, his in Illinois, where he had also been a merchant in the village of Cambridge. Retired in 1870, he was a man looking for new opportunities in land speculation and prospecting for minerals. It's uncertain when and exactly why he chose Cedar County, but it was sometime after 1875, when he was still listed on records in Cambridge. The 1880 Census listed him as a resident of Stockton.

- **James A. Cogle, 47,** the Indiana native who left an Arkansas teaching job to join the Union Army in 1861 had moved to Cedar County after the war. Taking up politics as well as farming, he had been active in both Cedar County and Stockton governments. He was the chairman of Stockton's Board of Trustees in 1868 when it passed the town's first ordinance prohibiting the use of firearms within the city limits, and the Cedar County superintendent of buildings who prepared plans for a new jail in 1871. Like Joseph Carrico Sr. and Morris Mitchell, he was known and respected throughout Cedar County.

- **James K. Peer, 37,** the Virginia farm boy had enlisted in the Confederate Army at age 18 in his father's place and served from 1863 through the end of the war. He'd been farming in Benton Township for 14 years when Jerico was organized. Besides being among the first to build in Jerico, he would provide key leadership 22 years later when fires nearly destroyed the town. In 1871, he had married Sarah Carrico, daughter to one Joe Carrico and sister to the other.

- **Joseph P. Brasher, 33**, who'd arrived in Benton Township in 1857 at age 7, had gone off to college, gotten an M. D. from the University of Nashville and a further degree from the Missouri Medical School in St. Louis. He returned to Benton Township in 1874 to practice and to marry Laura Mitchell, Morris Mitchell's daughter. The best educated of the group, his medical rounds took him over a wide area around the future town and a pleasing personality made him popular.

- **Charles Whitsitt, 33,** was a farmer and former store clerk when he arrived just before the town was laid out. A native of Kentucky who'd been in Western Missouri since age 12, he was essentially a stranger to the others though it seems certain he and Dan Stratton had discussed plans for a town before Mr. Whitsitt bought property immediately west of that Mr. Stratton bought when he acquired the springs.

- **Joseph B. Carrico Jr.**, who turned 25 in 1881, was the youngest among them and less is known of him pre-Jerico than any of the others. Listed as a farmer on the 1880 Census, he apparently was educated well beyond the one-room school level. He demonstrated advanced talent by designing the first Methodist Church and overseeing its construction in 1884. He proved himself an innovative merchant and civic leader, once designing an "egg wagon" to more safely transport Jerico's considerable egg exports to the rail stations in Lamar and Sheldon. He opened a store in Jerico shortly after Mr. Cogle and would remain central to Jerico's business affairs for the next quarter century.

It amounts to little more than rank speculation but a case can be made that Joe Carrico Sr. and Morris Mitchell served as the aged and wise counselors to the group; that Dan Stratton and Charles Whitsitt, ably abetted by Joe Carrico Jr. and Dr. Brasher, were the full-of-ideas men, though Mr. Whitsitt could also be grouped with James Peer and James Cogle as straight-ahead, first-things-first guys.

There is no speculation about two things: They were all doers and they were all put-your-money-where-your-mouth-is guys. There is no record of the financial resources brought to bear in Jerico's creation, but clearly Jerico's founders had money available to invest, to bet on themselves.

1870 assets of Jerico's founders*	
Daniel Stratton	$178,000
James Cogle	$162,000
Morris Mitchell	$116,000
J. B. Carrico Sr.	$109,000
C. E. Whitsitt	$18,000
James Peer, J. P. Brasher. not listed. J. B. Carrico Jr. 14 years old	
*In 2021 $$	
Source: 1870 U. S. Census	

The 1870 Census' list of respondents' assets showed four of the men could be classed as moderately well off at the time. Charley Whitsitt, then a 23-year-old-store clerk, had little. Given their natures and ambitions, the eight no doubt had improved their financial standings in the 12 years before Jerico was founded.

As the story goes, Daniel Stratton provided the spark. Suffering from some ailment lost to history, he had been told the waters of Carrico Springs could help. He found relief there and planned a town.

4. Founders

Daniel Stratton is clearly THE founder of Jerico Springs. He bought the land upon which it was built, he had it surveyed, he filed and signed the plat, along with his wife, Emily, and he promoted it.

Just as clearly, he did not do it all alone. The seven others listed as "founders" in this work are designated as such because they made important contributions at the founding and regularly appear in the record thereafter.

Sparse as the written record is, the visual one is more so. No photographs of Mr. Stratton, James K. Peer or Dr. Joseph Brasher could be found.

Pictures of the others that are available follow.

Joe Carrico Jr. holds the horse while a photographer got this late 1890s shot of his extended family in the buggy, including his father, Joe Carrico Sr.

Charles Whitsitt in later years, left, and at about the time Jerico was founded.
(Photos from Dr. Bill Neale collection)

Morris Mitchell and his wife, Mary Jane, (nee Lindley), in a photo likely taken sometime in the 1880s. The two were married Sept. 28, 1848, when he was 27 and she was 17. In 1850, he left her and their infant son in Missouri while he and her brother, James, joined the California gold rush. After his return two years later, the two, boosted by as many as eight slaves, built a prosperous farm near the future site of Jerico. But he left again in 1861 and spent four years at war as a captain in the Confederate Army. All they owned but the land itself was lost or destroyed during the war but the two had regained their prosperity by the time he assisted in launching Jerico in 1881-82.

James A. Cogle was a school teacher, a soldier, a politician and a farmer before turning to store keeping in Jerico. He opened the town's first retail outlet.

5. Assessing possibilities

There are no records of the 1881 discussions among the eight men and their neighbors, friends and families as they pondered and debated Daniel Stratton's ideas and, in the end, cast their lots together in a new town. But the core group comprised practical and ambitious men of impressive collective experience and the actions they undertook suggest they talked about transportation, mineral resources, retailing, marketing, education and competition, particularly in the healing-springs business.

There was plenty of the latter. More than 80 springs with reputed medicinal properties were scattered around Missouri alone, several with well-established resorts and more being built. El Dorado Springs, 20 miles to the north, and Zodiac Springs six miles to the west, were founded around mineral springs in 1881 even as Mr. Stratton and associates made their plans.

Still, demand was heavy. "Taking the waters" was at peak popularity in the U. S. during the last quarter of the 19th Century and people were traveling considerable distances to do so. Neither Daniel Stratton nor his associates, it became clear, feared competition of any sort. The first step would be selecting the right name to market. Mr. Stratton picked "Fountain of Youth." What better? Especially when coupled with guarantees of cures for rheumatism, piles (hemorrhoids) dropsy (edema) and a half-dozen other common ailments.

Transportation undeniably would be a major obstacle for people wishing to visit the springs. Roads for many miles in every direction were little beyond dirt and rock trails with many more fords than bridges. A railroad, though, would solve that problem and there was good reason for hope on that front. Sheldon, 16 miles to the west, was founded that very year as a point on the railroad line expanding south out of Kansas City. Lockwood, 20 miles to the south, also was founded in 1881 as a railroad point on tracks being laid northwest from Springfield into Kansas.

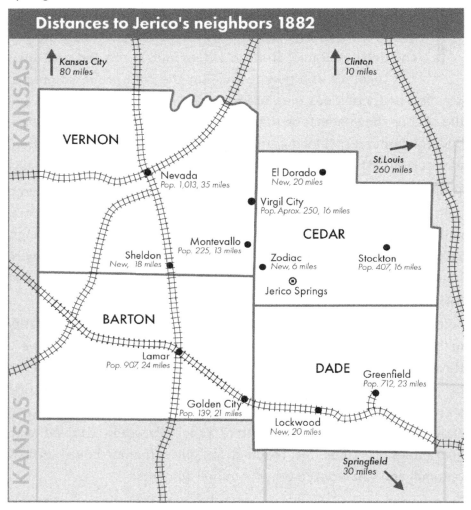

That Jerico's founders saw the expanding rail system as certain to pass through their town soon is readily understandable.

American railroading, barely 50 years old when Jerico was founded in 1882, was the wonder of the age in ways 21st Century man with his near-endless choices of transportation has trouble grasping.

Nineteenth Century man, though, had no trouble at all understanding what was before him: The rail system simply exploded. By 1880, two years before Jerico was founded, there were 93,200 miles of track in the nation, though none of it was very close to the future town.

The nearest service was 35 miles away, at Nevada, where a line south out of Kansas City ended in a junction with an east-west route connecting southeastern Kansas with Clinton and north central Missouri. Another route out of Clinton ran south to Springfield but was too far east to be helpful.

The railroad construction that led to Sheldon and Lockwood being founded in 1881 was the leading edge of a building binge that added 70,400 miles of track to the nation's system during the decade. The national confidence and optimism driving that unprecedented surge was reflected in Jerico's planners, themselves confident and optimistic men who saw rail service as much more than a mere means of bringing additional visitors to a health resort.

Jerico, they reasoned, could be an agricultural hub, an education beacon and, given the natural resources, a mining and manufacturing center. A mining company was formed even as the town was planned. The "Southwest Missouri Prospecting and Mining Company" was reported to have $150,000 ($3.8 million in 2021) behind it.

Beyond question, an enormous belt of good coal ran through southwestern Cedar County and large sections of Dade and Barton counties. The new town, too, would be on the northern fringe of the rich lead and zinc belt that was creating Joplin and a half-dozen other cities over three states. There was said to be iron ore north of the town site, too. Cedar County had it "in large quantities," according to that 1874 *Campbell's Missouri Gazetteer*, which also said, "in 1839 and 1840 a forge and furnace were built on Little Sac River and considerable iron of fair quality was made but the low prices and distance from market rendered the business unprofitable."

All these resources could be exploited with the arrival of rail service, which would also open new markets to the area's farmers, particularly needed by the fruit growers and their bountiful but time-sensitive produce. Jerico's planners also reasoned the railroads would be eager to serve such a resource-rich route.

The resulting city, the Jerico men believed, could rank among the leading in the region.

The group realized there was, meanwhile, opportunity as well as problems lurking in the poor transportation system. By 1880, Benton Township had grown to 1,643 people; Cedar County had passed 10,000. Benton Township's neighbors in Barton and Dade counties were growing as well.

All told, the town under discussion would be roughly in the middle of more than 400 square miles of small farms that had little retail service beyond itinerant salesmen and the occasional crossroads hamlet - places like Montevallo, Tingley, Sylvania and Filley - where a farm family could find a few choices in basic food, clothing and hardware items, and maybe a blacksmith. For more, there were long trips over poor roads to Stockton or Nevada or maybe Lamar or Greenfield.

All the people discussing a new town, the core eight and those among their neighbors joining in, would have understood in a very personal way how welcome a well-supplied retail center would be, as would be the attendant services, from barbers to blacksmiths. They also would have known that a good many of the farmers in that vast countryside were doing quite well, and calculated correctly they could make money as merchants despite the additional transportation costs to be incurred getting many of the goods to the town without rail service.

For all the big dreams and ambitions being laid out, Jerico's future depended first upon the farmers of Benton Township.

6. *The Mystic City rises*

D aniel Stratton, later called "a man of action" by the *Lamar Democrat*, moved quickly once he'd decided his course. He'd bought the land around the springs and he and Charley Whitsitt took the next steps, likely starting sometime in mid- to late 1881. They cleaned up the area around the springs, probably improving drainage, installing walkways and otherwise easing access.

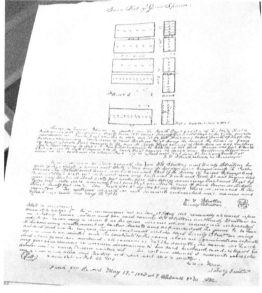

The plat of Jerico Springs, as filed by Daniel and Emily Stratton, May 17, 1882

They marked off a city block around the springs for the park they intended as the town's centerpiece. They planted trees on the prairie hillside, to shade the park.

Working with a surveyor, they laid out streets and lots, most likely finishing the work shortly before the "Town Plat of Jerico Springs," containing about 100 lots in eight blocks, was filed May 17, 1882, with the Cedar County recorder of deeds. Mr. Stratton and his wife, Emily, both signed the document.

Mr. Stratton left no written record of why he chose the name but he is probably the source for the locally accepted story that the "Jer" comes from the Biblical city of Jericho and the "ico" from Joseph Carrico Sr. In any case, the small stream wandering through town was soon called the Jordan and the hillside across from downtown, Jerusalem.

The Goodspeed *History* says "the first nail was driven in Jerico" on June 9, 1882. The building was Mr. Whitsitt's house, which had been dismantled and moved from his farm into Jerico, to a lot across the street south of the site of the future Methodist Church. It was reconstructed beginning June 9, celebrated as Founders Day for well more than a century with the widely attended Jerico Picnic that routinely drew multiples of the town's population.

The half-block deep, two-story brick building in the upper right was James A. Cogle's "Bee Hive" general merchandise store, Jerico's first retail outlet. The building, at the northeast corner of Main and Broadway, was later Joe Carrico Jr.'s "Little Acorn" department store. In 1905, Mr. Carrico sold the building to the Bank of Jerico, which undertook a major remodeling. It served three different banks before burning March 4, 1927.

Mr. Whitsitt turned his re-assembled house to use as a hotel and Jerico was in business.

Business boomed. Charley Whitsitt's house/hotel was quickly overwhelmed and people camped out in the hills around the springs just as they were doing in even greater numbers in the new town of El Dorado Springs, 20 miles north. The second house built in Jerico also was pressed into service as a hotel.

 Lots sold quickly and Mr. Stratton goosed growth by giving some away. Mr. Cogle's general merchandise store, called The Bee Hive, a two-story brick structure at the northeast corner of Broadway and Main, opened shortly after Mr. Whitsitt's hotel. Mr. Peer's United States Hotel eased the room shortage when it opened later in 1882, most likely at the northwest corner of Main and Park streets, where one or another hotel has stood throughout Jerico's existence.

Other business houses were springing up. Besides Mr. Peer and Mr. Cogle, several farmers near or at the site of Jerico made the transformation into merchants. Mr. Cogle, who with his sons and various partners operated several businesses for more than a decade, was soon followed into business by Hood Shumate, who also owned land at the site and who operated a variety of stores off and on for years. Joe Carrico Jr.'s general store, operated in partnership with Charles Sheppard, another farmer, soon joined the line-up.

Other early businesses, according to the Goodspeed *History*, included James Rogers & Co., Legg & Heiter, Clayton & Co., and Stratton & Lakey. The latter was a drug store (The Stratton was not Daniel); the others were general merchandise stores.

The Benton Township farmers turning to town careers were soon joined by outsiders looking to capitalize. Among them was Fred Neumann, from Phillips County in far northwestern Kansas, who arrived in late 1882. In April, 1883, the *Phillips County Freeman* noted that the local resident had requested his paper be sent in future to Jerico, where he "was building a large hotel." The Neumann House, a two-story wooden hotel at the top of Broadway overlooking the town and park, served Jerico for a quarter century under several different owners.

Another newcomer helped with the next critical resort amenities in early 1883 when M. J. Straight, from the Aurora area, joined Mr. Stratton in opening bathhouses where individual rooms offered places to take the waters, heated or cool, in private.

Mr. Straight, who like Mr. Stratton also took up prospecting, advertised widely that he "guaranteed in writing" that visitors to his "Fountain of Youth Bath House" would be cured of rheumatism, kidney disorders, blood poisoning and a half dozen other conditions so long as patients followed post-care instructions. He also advertised he would ship bottled Jerico water "anywhere in the U. S."

Additionally, Mr. Straight later operated a hotel, the Hilsabeck, where guests could "rent by the day or the week and the table is supplied with the best in the market."

Though it's uncertain exactly when this two-story brick building at the southwest corner of Main and Broadway went up, it was among the earliest in Jerico. The owners were CharleyWhitsitt, who used the left half, and Joseph Morris, who used the right half. The depiction is a line-drawing from the May 5, 1889 Jerico Spring Optic.

A third newcomer, Joseph Morris, partnered with Charley Whitsitt to put up a large two-story brick building at the southwest corner of Main and Broadway, facing Spring Park across Broadway. Mr. Morris, born in England in 1831, was listed as a miner in Michigan in the 1870 Census and as a "coal mine operator" in Illinois in 1880. He used the west half of the building for the "New York Store," presumably a general merchandise outlet. Given his background, he likely was involved in mining efforts as well.

Mr. Whitsitt used the east half of the building for his various ventures, including his real estate business.

Hartsong & Son added a flour mill that first year, just months after Jerico was laid out. An essential piece of farm country infrastructure, a mill provided both a market for grain and a place where it could be converted to flour for home use. Jerico would have one and sometimes two mills for most its first 40 years.

Hardware stores, drug stores, dry goods stores, grocery stores and general merchandise stores were the most common outlets of the time and Jerico soon had a selection of each, including the Peer & Brown hardware and implement store owned by J. W. C. Brown and James Peer, who was quick to expand beyond the hotel business.

Jerico early on acquired two key accoutrements of a real town: a post office and a newspaper.

Mr. Whitsitt was named Jerico's first postmaster Aug. 15, 1882, though he was replaced less than a month later by Mr. Cogle. (Each held the job several times over the next decade, an era when the job was openly political patronage.)

About the time the post office was established, Col. A. M. Crockett moved over from Nevada with a printing press and launched the *Jerico News.* It survives only in a handful of stories reprinted in other towns' papers but those provide further insight into Jerico's early growth.

The first, reprinted in the Oct. 5, 1882 *Dade County Advocate* in Greenfield, about 25 miles southeast of Jerico, confirms a building boom was on four months after Jerico was created.

"A big lumber merchant" from South Greenfield had visited Jerico and the News office, the story said. The merchant, T. A. Miller, wanted it known he'd just gotten in "20 carloads of lumber at unusually low prices" and, the story said, would "make it in the interest of all those who contemplate building in Jerico to buy their timber from him."

An Oct. 2, 1883 News story made it all the way to St. Louis and into the Globe-Democrat and thus to its enormous audience. The story reports the "Southwestern Mining Company" of Jerico was sinking shafts in Cedar, Dade and Greene counties. The company, made up of "some of the most reliable citizens of Cedar and Dade Counties," had $150,000 ($3.8 million in 2020) behind it, the News said.

Answering a question from the News editor, the unnamed company representative, said. "Our deepest shaft is about 25 feet and we have encountered gold, silver and copper in sufficient quantities to pay for the digging."

The St. Louis story greatly expanded the reach of the local mining stories, including one in the *Dade County Advocate* in September of 1883, several weeks earlier. The *Advocate* said the "Southwest Missouri Prospecting and Mining Company" was a "regular organized company with headquarters in Jerico."   Dr. J. K. Longacre, the company's secretary, told the Advocate there were "assays on all their works equal to Colorado or any other country."

With stories like those circulating, along with those about the wonders of the Fountain of Youth, it's little wonder growth exploded. Jerico's population hit 500 within 17 months, according to a story in the Oct. 14, 1883 Jefferson City *People's Tribune*, in the state capital.

The short story offered no source for the population figure. It said, "Jerico Springs, sixteen miles from Stockton, in Cedar County, is the latest youth restorer discovered. A town has been laid out with a population of 500. The water is said to be good for the piles."

Whatever the exact population, there are hints that Jerico witnessed some of the usual boom town problems; indeed, that it could be a very tough place.

The *Clinton Advocate* of April 12, 1883, reported the contents of a letter received in Clinton by the brother of the Jerico marshal. It said a man named Dean, who lived with his wife in a tent in Jerico, upon hearing he was to be arrested confronted the marshal, a gun in each hand. Bystanders quickly intervened. Dean left the store building where the confrontation occurred but soon returned "to kill" the marshal, he declared. The marshal, now armed with a double barrel shotgun, "would have killed him then and there, but Dean's wife appeared and on her account they did not hurt him," the letter said.

But a warrant for Dean's arrest was issued and the marshal sent the constable and a posse to serve it. Dean was not at his tent but the searchers eventually found him asleep in a haystack. They shot him and left him for dead, the letter recounted, though Dean the next morning crawled a quarter mile for help and was still alive when the letter was written.

Another hint that it was a tough town came in the Aug. 22, 1902 story in the *Jerico Optic* about the demolition the Rogers Block, comprising two store fronts and a second story hall on Main Street. "If the old building could talk, it could tell some hair-raising tales of the early days of Jerico Springs," the story said. "In the hall of this old structure occurred during its palling days one of the biggest fights, knife cuttings and general knock outs of any town in the state."

Ill side effects aside, the fast growth brought Jerico another key business in March of 1884 when the 22-month-old town got a bank. Organized by and named after John E. Hartley, a Stockton entrepreneur and banker, the Hartley Bank of Jerico Springs nevertheless was primarily financed and controlled by Jerico people.

The key figure was Dr. Brasher. Now 34, he and his wife, Laura, were among the town's first residents and he served on the first council. Named vice president of the bank, Dr. Brasher would later be its single largest stockholder, if he wasn't already.

A. M. Pyle, the president, a rural Jerico resident who raised livestock, was reputed to be among the wealthiest men of the region. Other stockholders included J. B. Carrico Sr., Morris Mitchell and Daniel Stratton, along with Joseph Morris, who was partnering in a major building with Charley Whitsitt. The bank had $11,000 in capital stock ($292,000 in 2020), and its depositors soon provided a welcome infusion of cash into a new town busy putting up buildings and assembling stocks of merchandise.

Sometime in early 1885, Mr. Whitsitt led planning for a major promotional effort that again demonstrated the town's leaders were thinking well beyond a health resort. A barbeque and exposition featuring local products and minerals was scheduled for Aug. 11. Speakers from as far away as Lawrence, Kan., were arranged. An invitation was extended to everyone.

It was a sophisticated approach to gaining publicity and it paid off in many ways, especially when the *Kansas City Times* dispatched a correspondent to cover it. The *Times* was read everywhere in Missouri and most places in Kansas. Getting its attention was a major public relations triumph.

The event was pretty much everything for which Mr. Stratton, Mr. Whitsitt and the others could have hoped, despite a torrential rainstorm that interrupted preparations and travel.

So was the *Times* story, for both its richly detailed picture of the event and the correspondent's declaration that "instead of a backwoods old styled class of people as we expected to see, we have not seen a more intelligent gathering anywhere in the state. "

The story ran under the headline "An Old Fashioned Barbeque": (Ellipses at a few points indicate an unreadable word.)

"JERICO SPRINGS, Mo., Aug. 11 – The anxiously awaited barbeque day came as announced today. Your correspondent was on the grounds yesterday and visited the area where some

fifteen fat cattle, sheep and hogs were being roasted over beds of coals on long trenches dug in the ground. The trenches had been filled with wood and burned down to a bed of coals, and the meat was suspended over the fire by many hickory poles held across. The meat was cooked as nicely as if it had been in the oven. Men were busy turning, carving and carrying meat to and fro. Hammers and saws were heard on every hand. Long tables were built and … men and swing men were busily engaged erecting their stands for the next day.

"Wagons were rushing to and from the grove hauling extra … on the grounds. Wagons and buggies loaded with strangers from a distance began to roll in about 5 o'clock and continued until late at night. Every hotel was full. Everything bid fair to be the grandest time ever in Cedar County. But about midnight rain began to fall in torrents and continued with little abatement till 9:30 in the morning. Every branch and stream of any size was out of banks, the streets were muddy and everybody was discouraged.

"The lemonade men and the swing men who had made great preparations were fairly making things blue swearing. However, about 10 o'clock, the clouds broke away, the sun came out and in less than an hour every road leading to town was lined with wagons. The meat committees had carefully kept the meat dry and revived their fires that had been extinguished by the rain and began to finish their work.

"By 11 o'clock 540 wagons had come into town and filled every available space for quite a distance around.

"At least 2,500 people had assembled and as many more were waiting on opposite sides of Cedar and Horse creek, unable to cross for the high water.

"Large delegations were out of Lamar, Milford, Nevada, Stockton, Lockwood and El Dorado.

"The first exercise was a well-timed address of welcome by Cedar's young orator, Isaac M. Porter, after which the people were quietly and orderly marched to the tables that were already spread with meals. Two huge wagon loads of light bread were driven up to the tables and everybody was fed and many took loaves away. A member of the provisions committee told me they had about 200 loaves of bread left.

"After dinner, the I.O.O.F. and G.A.R. societies formed a grand procession and march from town to the grounds, making a brilliant display. Speeches were made by Elder J. B. Carrico and Rev. R. W. Reynolds. Speakers cut off by high water, were Judge D. M. Wooldridge, Hon. C. M. Morgan and Captain R. J. Tucker of Lawrence.

"A display of products, etc., of Cedar county was arranged. A massive cut stone speaker's table was on the stand, cut out of Jerico stone by R. C. Laing of Jerico. On this table was a stone urn in which was a beautiful bouquet. At the right of the speaker's stand at which a huge 5-bushel lump of coal from Moore's bank, a mile and a half south of Jerico. It measured 32 inches thick by my own tape lines. It was of very fine quality and attracted marked attention. To the left of the stand was a display of silk ... by Mrs. J. B. Bowman of Jerico. It showed all the stages from the eggs up to cocoons, spinning and reeling off of the raw silk. It was quite a curiosity to the people generally. In the rear of the speakers was a display of corn, millet, vegetables, fruit, sorghum and minerals equal to any county fair.

"The speaker's ... consisted of a large flagstone, 24x56 inches and smooth as a board.

"Cedar county may be called behind, and her soil may not be ruled rich, but Wednesday's display has convinced thousands of her merits, and shown her to have a productive soil not to be excelled by any other county in the state. Her resources have never been developed. And before 12 months rolls around, she will have a railroad to help her make a marked development.

"We would fail to do justice if we did not mention that instead of a backwoods old styled class of people as we expected to see, we have not seen a more intelligent gathering anywhere in the state. Their hospitality is unbounded.

"We must congratulate such men as J. F. Rogers, C. E. Whitsitt, G. W. Smith and W. R. Hast for the meal and untiring energy displayed in carrying out the programme and making it a perfect success under the attending circumstances.

"After all the mishaps it was an enjoyable occasion."

Pulling off the event, which drew more than five times the town's population, demonstrated a high degree of community cooperation and a willingness to pick up the substantial tab for feeding thousands of visitors. It also demonstrated, again, the confidence and optimism residing in Charley Whitsitt, Dan Stratton and others of the town's leading men.

The exposition and other promotional efforts continued to pay dividends in growth. Housing shortages plagued the town. On Dec. 5, 1885, the Macon Republican in north-central Missouri reported, "Jerico has more families coming in than she can provide housing for and is now urging upon people the necessity of starting a saving and loan association."

Such an association was launched, with Charley Whitsitt as secretary, but the housing shortage persisted throughout the 1880s. "Jerico needs 20 more dwelling houses to keep up with the demand from immigration," the Dec. 19, 1889 *Stockton Journal* reported.

Jerico continued concrete advances toward other goals. Williams and Legg Company opened a fruit evaporator in 1886. Another basic farm country service, the evaporator provided a means of drying the area's substantial fruit crop for home storage or a trip to market. The company secretary? Charley Whitsitt.

Sometime in the mid to late 1880s, the All Purpose Harrow Company began manufacturing its product in Jerico. The company advertised its harrow, a common farm implement, as light weight and able to work effectively in rocky ground. A. C. Beck, who owned well more than 400 acres west of Jerico, was identified in the ad as the man to contact for the product or for a sales territory.

The ubiquitous Charley Whitsitt was "connected" to the company. His own Whitsitt and Company now included a lumber yard.

Mr. Whitsitt also made what proved to be his most lasting contribution to Jerico in 1887, when his wife, Annie, 36, died. He provided a tract of land at the southeast corner of town for a cemetery and named it Anna Edna in her honor. It still serves Jerico.

Two years later, he married Laura Morris, daughter of Joseph Morris, with whom he partnered in several business ventures.

7. So far, so good

Daniel Stratton was surely in an expansive and satisfied mood on Christmas Day 1887 when he and his wife, Emily, hosted "a splendid reception and dinner for a number of friends at the Barker Hotel." The guests most certainly would have included at least some of the others who'd invested their money and nearly six years of their lives in Jerico. They all were entitled to some satisfaction with their accomplishments and to some optimism about the future of their creation.

Where open prairie had existed just six years earlier, Jerico was a thriving retail and service center – its core area around Spring Park on Main, Broadway and Park streets offered nearly five full blocks of business establishments. Manufacturing was taking hold. New addition after new addition by Mr. Stratton, Mr. Whitsitt and by Mr. Stratton with various other partners had pushed Jerico to nearly a full square mile in area, much of it covered with homes, existing or under construction.

New business buildings and remodeled ones were up or in progress, including the Pickett Block, a two-story brick building stretching for a half block along Main Street at the southeast corner of Main and Broadway.

There were five churches, a literary society, an active temperance union, chapters of the Masons, the International Order of Odd Fellows, Woodmen of the World, and the Grand Army of the Republic. There was a thriving social scene featuring house parties, school plays, traveling speakers and lecture series, community meals, plays horse races and outings to fish and camp along Horse and Cedar creeks or Sac River.

The population was somewhere around 500, close to or even exceeding that of Stockton, the much older county seat. El Dorado's boom, it was true, had outstripped Jerico's, but all seemed still on the upswing for their town as the Strattons entertained their guests.

Whatever disappointment attended the dinner would have been the failure to have secured a railroad.

Jerico's men had been trying. The few stories available show them fully engaged in the effort, perhaps beginning to understand how slippery railroad men could be.

The 1885 Kansas City Times story about the barbeque/exposition had said without any specifics or a source that a railroad would run through Jerico "within 12 months." That didn't happen but there were at least two irons in the fire in 1887.

On June 16, the *Lamar Missourian* reported that Dr. Brasher had been in St. Louis and secured an interview with the president, attorney and three directors of the proposed St. Louis and Colorado Railroad Co. The men informed Dr. Brasher, the story said, "that Lamar would certainly be a point on the road though they could not promise him as to Jerico."

On Sept. 15, 1887, the *Hermitage Index* said Jerico was making an effort to raise $25,000 ($684,000 in 2021) to secure a depot on the proposed Chicago, Jefferson City, Girard and El Paso road. The same issue of the *Index* carried a *Jerico News* story that said surveyors for the road were likely to be in town the next week and urged readers to make them welcome.

It was the *Hermitage Index*, too, that earlier in the year explained the uncertain terrain occupied by railroad promoters and the towns with which they were locked in mutually hopeful embraces.

The *Index* reported there were two surveys underway on the route through Jerico, one for the proposed Chicago to El Paso road and the other for the Santa Fe company, a long-established road with thousands of miles of track. Both roads were soliciting support from towns along the route. The *Index* editor warned that the Santa Fe was merely feinting, that if people threw support to it, thus killing the upstart new company and whatever competition it might offer, the Santa Fe would simply cancel its plans.

Therefore, the editor said, towns along the proposed route should ignore the Santa Fe and support the new company that was serious about building a road. Jerico took that advice and tried to raise the $25,000 to guarantee a station on the proposed Chicago to El Paso route.

Tricky competition aside, the explosion in track building continued and there seemed little reason to doubt eventual success for Jerico. In the meantime, regular hack services hauled people, mail and light goods to and from train stations in Sheldon, Lamar and Lockwood, and teamsters provided the link for heavier loads.

8. 1888: Hustle, bustle and hope

As 1888 arrived, Jerico was a thriving, bustling place full of shoppers and visitors, with new construction all about.

A good picture of life that year is provided by whomever wrote the "Jerico Jottings" column in the weekly *Stockton Journal*. Working under the nom de plume "Hoosier," his (or her) account of life in the "mystic city" - Hoosier's frequently used synonym for Jerico - is a collection of one-sentence strokes that paint a picture of a vibrant town full of people of wide-ranging interests, considerable civic pride and intellectual curiosity.

A selection:

In his first report of the year, on Jan. 5, Hoosier reports the "college students are returning and there are more of them." The report serves to establish that there was a college taking students at least as early as 1887.

Hoosier also reported that week he (assuming he was a man) was "proud to state that one Christmas and New Year had passed without drinking and drunkenness in Jerico. Credit to the W.C.T.U."

In the same column, Hoosier reported the school's holiday vacation had been prolonged for a week because of a measles and mumps outbreak; that the Loyal Temperance Legion had given an "excellent literary entertainment;" and that the struggling Jerico News had "gone into winter quarters. Whether the return of the daises will revive its torpidity, we can't say."

The economic news was mostly good though. Several farms had been sold the past few weeks, a mule buyer had been through town and "distributed considerable cash among our farmers," year-end inventories showed many merchants had a good 1887 and the coming building season was expected to be the busiest yet in Jerico.

Hoosier reported in February that "real estate sales were quite lively, according to Dan Stratton" and that a man named W. A. Cleveland would soon add "a first-class grocery store ... to the mystic city."

In March, E. D. Pickett was in town to make arrangements "for the full completion of his brick block." He would do so and the half-block long two-story brick structure at the southeast corner of Main and Broadway would house several important retail outlets until it was destroyed by fire June 5, 1904.

Hoosier noted that Mr. Theodore Kerr, of Little Rock Ark., in town scouting business opportunities, was said to have settled on starting a newspaper to replace the *Jerico News,* which indeed had failed to come out of winter quarters. The *Jerico Springs Optic*, launched by Mr. Kerr in March, would last 49 years.

March, 1888, was otherwise a busy month. Hoosier's accounts:

"Whitsitt & Wimer last week sold right at 1,000 acres of Cedar county land to northern and eastern men." (Charley Whitsitt and T. T. Wimer were principals in the company.)

"J. R. Duncan, a grocery merchant of this city, shipped to Kansas City 2,400 dozen eggs and it was not an extra good week for eggs."

"A. M. Pyle, our Benton township cattle king, last Thursday sold to Mr. Sieg, of Bates County, 40 head of three-year-old steers which brought $1,325.00 ($36,000 in 2020)."

"Again, a large brick hotel and sanitarium is talked of as one of the future enterprises for the mystic city, and which we hope will materialize in the near future." (It didn't.)

Also in March, F. A. Brasher, Dr. Brasher's brother and also a stockholder in the Hartley Bank, was called to Jefferson City to serve on a federal court jury. While there, he arranged an interview with "the governor and several other important officials and assured them Jerico was among the solid cities of our great state."

As the year progressed, Dr. Brasher "added a powerful microscope to his well selected store of surgical instruments," and "gradually turned more of his attention to the breeding of fine horses."

D. H. Shumate and J. A. Cogle put "a neat brick sidewalk in front of their business houses;" and "Everybody has planted out trees this spring, which adds materially to be appearance of our town."

More from Hoosier in 1888:

"Several very able speakers of the Labor Party addressed a full house here last Saturday. With slight exceptions, they would make good Democrats."

"Our new village trustees propose adopting general sidewalk ordinances, which move will be heartily approved by our citizens."

"D. G. Stratton has at last finished the long list of improvements on his residence property and now again has one of the neatest homes in the city."

"Metz & Grubbs have commenced molding brick for a new kiln, although they have a kiln of 100,000 left over from last season. They also propose manufacturing tile on a large scale this season."

"Our mill proprietors are talking of putting in rollers at an early date."

"M. F. Daniels this week purchased D. C. Johnson's interest in the Cogle & Johnson dry goods store."

"Stratton & Lakey have put down a neat brick sidewalk on the two fronts of their drugstore." (The drug store Stratton was not Daniel.)

"A. B. Stratton, W. R. Lakey and J. W. Lakey are each adding neat verandas to their dwellings."

"Our citizens along Broadway and Main streets are busy putting down sidewalks."

"The young folks enjoyed a very pleasant time at an ice cream party at J. K. Peer's."

"A singing school is now one of the evening attractions for our young people."

"A company of our citizens are now busily engaged sinking a shaft for lead, which they feel confident they will find at a reasonable depth."

"The hacks of the Lamar and Jerico hack line have arrived here heavily loaded with passengers every day this week, and on Friday, were compelled to put on an extra hack in order to accommodate all."

"A horse race last Saturday between the Spotted Flyer, owned by Lafe Six, and a sorrel filly owned by Marion Welsh, was hotly contested on the track south of town. Result, 12 feet in favor of the filly."

"Our citizens very generally are repainting their houses and barns which gives a special freshness to the appearance of the mystic city."

In an item demonstrating the respect and stature an aging J. B. Carrico Sr. had achieved, Hoosier wrote, "Uncle Joe Carrico, our modern Ben Franklin, delivered a very interesting course of lectures here last week – subject, the rise and progress of reformation and the cause and cure of infidelity. It is needless to say that his subject was well handled."

The *Kansas City Times* took note of Jerico again, reporting in its July 4, 1888 issue, "Jerico is an interesting town and generally gets what it wants. Its new industry is a jelly works where the fine fruit of this section will be made into jelly, apple butter and cider."

If Mr. Stratton threw a holiday party as 1888 drew to a close, his outlook would have been little changed from 1887's. The bustling retail center and health resort remained a solid foundation on which to turn larger dreams into reality.

9. 1889: The dream enunciated

Those dreams were clearly enunciated by the newcomer Thomas L. Kerr, a 34-year-old New Jersey native who had arrived via Kansas and Arkansas in early 1888. He used his newly founded *Jerico Springs Optic* to loudly promote his new home, so much so that Daniel Stratton rewarded him with a lot said to be worth $500 ($13,500 in 2021).

Sometime in early 1889, certainly working in close consultation with Charley Whitsitt, Daniel Stratton and others in the town, Mr. Kerr put together a four-page supplement to the *Optic* in which he laid out the case for Jerico for anyone looking for a new home or business opportunity.

Published May 5, 1889, and widely distributed, Mr. Kerr's work is filled with hyperbole, exaggeration and a couple shaky leaps in logic, but at its core is a basically correct statement of what Jerico was, what it wanted to be and how it meant to get there. One of only two pre-1901 Optics to survive, the microfilm copy is difficult and sometimes impossible to read.

In the main story, Mr. Kerr declared, "It is evident to our mind that there is an opportunity to establish an important and wealthy city at this point, and it is with the desire that others may come and assist and share in the profits of our success that we place the reasons for a faith in Jerico Springs before our readers."

He then presented a list of 20 of those reasons, addressing each at least briefly. He mentioned, among others, soil types, water resources, timber, building stone, lead, coal, fruit, stock raising, natural gas and railroads – "Jerico has just as good a prospect for one or more railroads as any town could have and not actually have the road," he declared.

There was a list of most businesses in town and a long string of testimonials from people who'd found relief or cures at the springs as

44

well as a chemical analysis of the spring water and a list of ills it could sooth.

Mr. Kerr even recapped the previous year's first-fruit-and-vegetable stories, so that prospective residents knew that by the last week of April in 1888, the first wild gooseberries were in the markets and that strawberries were available; that Mrs. G. T. White had new potatoes for dinner May 11; that one day in mid-May a Jerico merchant paid out $65.66 in cash ($1,800 in 2020) for fresh produce; and that on June 1, the cherries were in the market.

Every argument made over the next 30 years in favor of Jerico was to some degree or another derivative of Mr. Kerr's work. The main story follows, or at least so much of it as is legible.

Jerico Springs

——-

Cedar County Mo., and the advantages offered to

——

Those in search of Health, Wealth and Happy Homes

——

A country where the raising of horses, mules, cattle and

——

Hogs yield large returns and grain growing is profitable

——

Jerico is a mining town – coal, iron, lead and zinc

—-

Strong evidence of natural gas and the probability that

——

Jerico will be the greatest manufacturing town in the west.

—–

Soft water, mild climate and

—–

the greatest Health resort in the world

—–

You are invited to come.

"In calling the attention of the home seeker to the numerous advantages of this section, we do so with the hope and expectation of increasing our population and developing our resources. Individually, we have no land to sell nor are we paid by anyone having land for sale, but this is our home because we firmly believe this country more healthy, pleasant and offering greater advantages to a man of limited means than any other place we know of.

"To accumulate a home and business in sections well developed requires the labor of years while here the task is comparatively easy. It is our desire to see this section thickly peopled, because then the resources in the country will be developed, better markets will be secured, and the property and business of each individual will be enhanced in proportions to his interest, and to the extent to which the section may be developed it is evident to our mind that there is a great opportunity to establish an important and wealthy city at this point, and it is with the desire that others may come and assist and share in the profits of our success that we place the reasons for a faith in Jerico Springs before our readers.

"Cedar County

"is situated in the second tier of counties east of Kansas and 4th North of the Arkansas line, and has an area of 480 square miles,

Ads from the May 5, 1889 Jerico Springs, Optic.

or 316,000 acres of land. Financially, the county is in as good a shape as any county in the West. The eastern half of the county is a timbered country with only a few small prairies; the western is mostly prairie, with belts of timber along the streams and beautiful groves on the highland in the distance resembling orchards more than groves of forest trees.

"The soil

"is red mulatto, black loam and white (unreadable). The red mulatto is adapted to the cultivation of fruit; an apple orchard planted on it never failed to produce a crop of apples. It is equally as good for wheat, potatoes, root vegetables, and clover and bluegrass find a congenial home in it. The alluvial soil is found in the river and creek bottoms and prairie valleys and is the farmer's favorite soil for corn, (unreadable) magnificent wheat crops are grown on land of this character. The black loam found principally on the broad prairies produce the heaviest drops of corn but wheat and all the grasses, vegetables and fruits, grow luxuriantly and attain the highest degree of perfection.

"Society

"Nearly every state in the Union is represented among the people of Cedar County and they comprise that class full of determination and an independent spirit. The people are moral, industrious and hospitable, and extend a (unreadable) welcome to all who come here to better their condition and assist in the development of the country.

"Timber

"Black and white walnut, white, black and shell bark hickory, blackjack, sugar tree, common maple, red bud, pawpaw, (unreadable), huckleberry, black and blue ash, birch, (unreadable), persimmon, wild cherry, sycamore, elm, hazel, box elder, (unreadable) mulberry and all the different species of oak

common to this latitude, (unreadable) the principal streams lined with cedar, from which our county derives its name.

"Building stone

"A very fine grade of building stone is found in Cedar County, a large quarry of which is found immediately north of Jerico. This stone is susceptible to artistic (unreadable), examples of which can be seen in any of the buildings of the city.

"Coal

"A body of coal 6 miles wide and 16 miles long has been developed in Jerico, that is, farmers have discovered coal and are using it for family purposes and to supply the coal trade from the extent of territory described. This coal is of the peacock variety, is harder than bituminous and softer than anthracite. It is the best coal for all purposes. In the west blacksmiths prefer it to the Pittsburgh, Kansas, coal even at an increased cost. The time when this section of Cedar County will become one of the greatest coal mining centers in the west is limited to the time when transportation facilities have been secured. at the present time Jerico supplies a number of neighboring towns with coal, but the lack of railroad transportation is a serious drawback to this industry, which will soon become one of the most important features of the country. The price of coal is $2 per ton at the mines. It will take generations to exhaust the supply even with the most extensive mining.

"Water

is found in the thousands of never-failing springs as pure as ever run from the Earth, and can be had nearly anywhere in the county, and as soft as rainwater by digging from 15 to 40 ft deep. The county is traversed by Bear, Cedar and Horse creeks, Big and Little Sac rivers running on the north and fed by springs furnishing an abundance of water power for propelling all kinds of machinery.

"Fruit

"This is peculiarly a fruit country. Apples, peaches, pears, cherries, grapes and in fact every kind of fruit peculiar to this climate, grows here in great abundance. Among the specimens of fruit brought to our offices by neighboring farmers were peaches measuring from nine to 10 inches in circumference; apples weighing from one to one and a half pounds each; and pears that measure 12 inches around one way and 13 in the other. In quantity and quality, we believe fruits of all kinds do better here than in any other section we know of. Wild fruits grow in abundance. To anyone willing to engage in raising fruit for profit we believe that this section offers the greatest inducements. Fruit never fails to yield a beautiful harvest here.

"Rye

is absolutely a safe crop and is equal to two ordinary crops, as it pays for its seed and sewing for fall, winter and spring pasturage, after which it yields a large crop of grain.

"Tobacco

"As fine tobacco as is produced in the United States (the (unreadable) regions of Virginia not excepted) can be grown here, and land considered only 2nd or 3rd class for common farm purposes is first class for tobacco and produces the finest and most valuable article in the great tobacco market of our country.

"Meadow

"Timothy, clover, red top, orchard grass, etc. succeed well wherever tried. In the settled portion of the county, where the raw grasses have been eaten out by stock, bluegrass is rapidly taken its place and air many years all our country that is not under cultivation will be unbroken bluegrass sward.

"Stock raising

"is the principal business, and the one from which our farmers at present derive the greatest amount of their income. Horses, mules, cattle, sheep and hogs are extensively raised and the short and mild winters, abundance of fine pasturage and the fact that buyers are always ready to buy all surplus stock makes this a superior country for the enterprising stock grower.

"Other crops

"Corn is the staple crop of the county. Wheat and oats are also largely raised. A complete failure of these crops was never known. There are some castor beans, flax and broom corn grown in the county.

"Lead and zinc

"Fine deposits of both lead and zinc have been found at various places near the city, but owing to the lack of sufficient capital, the owners have not developed them. Both of these industries will be extensively carried on after the necessary capital and transportation have been secured.

"Iron

North of the city there are immense deposits of iron ore and the closeness of large bodies of (unreadable) and coal will reduce the cost of production to a point (unreadable) competition with any portion of the United States. The first blast furnace will bring about a great at change in the future of Jerico as it did with the city of Birmingham.

"Health

"In regard to health this area has no superior. The water in this portion of the county is soft and pure and its use has cured many *cases of kidney disorders. There are no swamps or stagnant water and no malaria. The air is pure and wholesome and many people move their families here principally because of this great blessing.*

"Manufacturing

"Jerico is destined to become a great manufacturing center because a great variety of the raw materials needed in the arts and trades are found here in almost endless quantities. Food is raised in great abundance and the country very pleasant and one in which healthfulness is promoted. The All-Purpose Harrow factory is located at this place This is an institution which promises to grow into an extensive establishment.

Ads from the May 5, 1889 Jerico Springs Optic included one for the All Purpose Harrow Company, seen as the start of manufacturing in Jerico. Those in the right-hand column include several for stud services.

This implement will perform seven different kinds of farm work and is proclaimed by every farmer who sees it work to be the best harrow made. There is one large flowering mill, two brickyards and a tile factory.

"Natural gas

"There is no doubt about Jerico being underlain with natural gas, though not yet developed. The first incident going to prove this to be a fact happened several years ago when a citizen, Mr. (unreadable) Reynolds dug a cellar which the rains filled with water. Bubbles came to the surface, which on being lighted burned. The second proof was the discovery of gas in a well and coming through a fracture in the rock at the bottom which also burned. The third evidence consists in the following: The well just referred to was drilled to a depth of 143 feet. For 2 weeks, the drill passed through lead and zinc but owing to a lack of funds the work was abandoned and the well, which was located on a low piece of ground. allowed to be covered at by a small (unreadable). Daily and sometimes oftener, the water covering the mouth of this well is violently thrown into the air sometimes 15 feet high and wetting this rounding banks.

"Railroads

"Jerico has just as good a prospect for one or more railroads as any town could have and not actually have the road.

"The examination of the St Louis and San Francisco system will show that their lines extend from St Louis to Monett, Mo., and there it divides into three branches, one going south into Texas and there combining with the Pacific coast trades; another going west to the Indian Territory and still another going west of (unreadable) into Western Kansas. This vast system (unreadable) to Kansas City (unreadable) running through this city by extending the line from Monett to Kansas City it will connect the system with Kansas City in the most direct and practical manner. The route has been permanently located the entire distance and at no point does its grade exceed 50 feet to the mile, to which grade the engineers were limited. The proposed road which has

*located its route through this city is the Chicago, Jefferson City &
(unreadable), and this company has secured the right of way and
proposes to (unreadable) building early next spring.*

"Disadvantages

*"There is no portion of the world without disadvantages, some to
a greater and some to a less extent. The greater and only real
disadvantage that we can find for this country is the market. It is
true that fair prices are realized for livestock and grain, but fruit
and vegetables are ridiculously (unreadable) due to the great
abundance, limited local demand and inferior shipping facilities.
In less than a year, however, we will be only about 6 hours travel
from Kansas City." Three lines unreadable.*

"Advantages

*"Occasionally a man from (unreadable) country comes here and
at first objects to our hills. While we are to an extent surrounded
and protected by hills, they are few and (unreadable) to the
country of Jerico and in the opinions of the old settlers they are a
blessing instead of a drawback."*

The next 30 lines or so are unreadable.

*"... healthful and altogether the industrious and thrifty man with
small means will find here one of the best locations to be found
anywhere in the nation to make a home amid surroundings at
once delightful and furnishing the elements out of which industry
begets prosperity and leads to the happiness of those who adopt
the one and enjoy the other. The man who comes here from the
long dreary winters of Northern and Eastern States and saves
what he is compelled to spend there in extra preparations in no
way needful or profitable here, will be surprised to find how
rapidly the savings accumulate and how soon he has been able*

to place himself and family and into a position of comparative ease and comfort.

"This is undoubtedly one of the very best fruit sections of America. Our upland, which is the most adapted to fruit raising, can now be bought at less prices and on reasonable terms. Before the time this land can be set to fruit and brought to bearing, Jerico will the connected with Kansas City by rail and fruit delivered to the depot at Jerico will reach Kansas City in about 6 hours. The greater the number who engage in this business, the greater the public will be for better and cheap shipping facilities, and. in the demand for cheap fruit can never be satisfied. (unreadable) are here now making arrangements for this business and they are (unreadable) to have others join them."

Last three lines unreadable.

In addition to the railroad discussion in his main story, Mr. Kerr included these quotes from railroad promoters in a separate piece:

From Col. Bond of the proposed Kansas City, Monett and Southern railroad, "There is all the business our road can handle at Jerico Springs, from the very time we get in operation. And it is of a permanent nature."

From Col. Cauw, of the proposed Chicago, Jefferson City, Girard and El Paso road: "Jerico Springs will be one of the most important points on our line. Its natural resources far exceed those of any other section of the state of Missouri."

With men such as that saying things such as that, how could anyone doubt the track-laying crews would be appearing over the horizon any day?

Jerico, though was taking nothing for granted and when there was a meeting called in Nevada Nov. 7, 1889 to discuss yet another proposed road, the Kansas City, Nevada & Fort Smith (Ark.), Jerico sent Mr.

Whitsitt and A. C. Beck, the All Purpose Harrow Co. man, to represent it. Everyone was enthusiastic about the plan, the *Nevada Noticer* reported.

While it waited and worked on a railroad, Jerico moved ahead on other fronts. A concerted effort to establish a cannery was made early in 1889, with residents pledging $3,100 in cash and $700 in materials and labor ($107,500 in 2020) toward its construction. Several other towns, including Greenfield and El Dorado, were also eager to launch a cannery, which would "turn into money the vast quantity of fruit that now goes to waste," the *Greenfield Vedette* said Feb. 14.

Daniel Stratton continued his search for a big mining strike, investing in land near Golden City, where drills reaching 63 feet down encountered "18 feet of paying minerals, then a solid vein of lead," according to the Lamar Democrat. Neither cannery nor mine worked out in the end.

On a somewhat odd note, the oddly named *Sedalia Weekly Bazoo* reported in its Oct. 1, 1889 issue that it was clear Jerico was a huge success since it "has three first class butcher shops."

For all the high praise he heaped on Jerico in his May 5 issue of the *Optic*, Theodore Kerr moved on a month later. In early June, he sold the *Optic* to a man named G. M. Armstrong, who held it for but a few months before selling it to A. M. Heifner. Mr. Heifner had arrived in Jerico early in 1889 and operated a daily hack service between Jerico and Lamar before acquiring the *Optic*. He and his descendants would control the paper for virtually all its remaining 48 years. It would be a loyal promoter of the town for all that time.

One other 1889 arrival is noteworthy. E. R. Hightower, a young attorney native to Atchison County in Missouri's far northwestern corner, quickly settled into the real estate and insurance business. In time, his efforts to build Jerico would equal those of Mr. Stratton and Mr. Whitsitt.

Another name beginning to appear in the newspapers was that of F. M. Bruster, who'd arrived in Benton Township as a five-year-old a decade before Jerico was founded. Now in his late 20s, he was a popular school teacher who was active in county teacher organizations and, increasingly, Democratic politics. In 1890, the *Stockton Journal* called him "one of Cedar County's most prominent and influential teachers." He would play an ever-larger role in Jerico.

10. The women of Jerico

The women of Jerico play the traditional female role in history: Invisible in the record. That applies to the wives of the founders as well as to women in general.

When women's names do show up in the newspapers the stories most often concern their activity in such traditional roles as serving on church committees and as officers in organizations like the Women's Christian Temperance Union and literary societies. When the Jerico Literary Society was formed in 1889, Emma Longstreet was assistant secretary and Myrtle Peer was treasurer; the four other officers were men.

Women were frequently school teachers as well, though they mostly made appearances in newspapers only when they were hired somewhere for the following term.

Women in the business world were rare. When the *Stockton Journal* in 1889 ran a list of 75 or so Cedar County business owners paying county taxes, only three names were clearly those of women.

An 1893 list of the 62 people holding stock in Cedar County's five banks, included just one name clearly that of a woman. Sarah A. Sheppard held five of the 110 shares issued by the Hartley Bank of Jerico and valued at $500 ($15,000 in 2021). A remarkable woman, Sarah Sheppard was married to a large Benton Township landowner, Thomas Sheppard, when the Civil War broke out. The 1860 Census said he had $3,000 in real estate and $1,000 in personal property, the total equivalent to $128,000 in 2021 dollars.

Thomas joined the Union Army, leaving Sarah and six children ranging in age from 1 to 14 to fend with life in Benton Township. The *Cedar County Republican*, in its Nov. 1, 1900 obituary, said "Three or four times she mounted a horse and rode into Kansas to recover her cattle that had been stolen, accomplishing the feat with the tact and nerve of a true heroine."

Riding from Benton Township on through Vernon or Barton County into Kansas at that time would have a been a journey where violence and death lurked everywhere.

Thomas returned at war's end, his health shattered, and attempted to move the family to California. Their horses were stolen in Kansas and Thomas soon died. Sarah returned to Cedar County to rear her family. The 1870 Census said she was keeping a boarding house in Stockton but also reported she had $2,000 worth of real estate and $500 in personal property, or about $50,000 in 2021 dollars.

The *Republican* was certainly correct to say, "She had the characteristic fiber and spirit of the early settler, and occupies a large and glorious page in the history of Cedar county." For all the large and glorious page Sarah Sheppard wrote, however, the *Republican*'s editor didn't bother with her name. She was "Grandma Sheppard, widow of Thomas Sheppard."

One of her sons, Charles W. Sheppard, partnered with Joe Carrico Jr., in several business ventures from 1885 forward.

It was 1901 before another woman was listed as a bank stockholder. There were a half dozen more during the remaining years Jerico had banks, but none were ever a director or officer.

Running millinery shops, dress shops and cafes were the most common business roles for women, - Sarah Peer and Malissa Carrico, wives of founders James Peer and Joseph Carrico Jr. - both did so at various points. Malissa Carrico also frequently accompanied Mr. Carrico on trips to Kansas City and St. Louis to select stock for his Little Acorn Department store.

An 1893 directory of Jerico businesses listed four women, two milliners and two music teachers.

In 1908, a woman named Marry Kile opened a photo studio in Jerico. Though the *Optic* said she "has a new outfit and will do your work satisfactorily," her name does not show up again.

For the most part, though, there is little beyond the most basic life facts available about the women who were a part of creating Jerico. That is enough to know they included many people of extraordinary strength, courage and determination.

Eleanor Carrico accompanied Joe Carrico Sr. on that 500-mile journey into the 1840s wilderness of western Missouri, where neighbors were miles away and the nearest town was a small collection of log huts 16 miles distant. There, living with the daily struggle to keep a roof overhead and food on the table, she bore seven children over the next 12 years.

Then, as the 1860s and a degree of prosperity arrived, so did the Civil War. Eleanor Carrico was forced to watch as all she and Joe had created over nearly 20 years was destroyed or stolen. Ordered to leave Cedar County or be killed, the Carricos and many of their neighbors did so, many of them, probably including the Carricos, went all the way to Illinois to wait out the war.

Back in Missouri at war's end, Joe and Eleanor soon recreated the prosperity that had been destroyed and lived out their days comfortably. If any newspaper did her obituary, it does not survive.

The life of Mary Jane Mitchell, Morris' wife, is similar. Reared in Polk and Dade counties in the 1830s and '40s, she was 17 years old when she married 27-year-old Morris Mitchell in 1848. In 1850, she and their infant son stayed in Cedar County while he made the trek to the California goldfields. It seems likely she stayed with or nearby her parents for the two-plus years he was gone.

He apparently had some degree of success in California for upon his return, he began buying land near the site of future Jerico and slaves to work it. The 1860 Census reported the value of his land and personal property totaled about $500,000 in 2021 dollars, though about two-thirds of it was the value of eight slaves.

The arrival of the Civil War brought unspeakable hardship to Mary Jane Mitchell, as well as to Eleanor Carrico. Morris, a veteran of the Mexican War, joined the Confederate Army as soon as fighting began and served until war's end as a captain in a cavalry outfit. If Mary Jane saw him at all for the next four years, the visits would have been quick and furtive, for visiting soldiers from either side were sometimes murdered in bitterly divided Cedar County.

Mary Jane was left to tend to four children age 11 and under in what had become a savage and dangerous place. The order in which events occurred have been lost, but the Mitchells' home was burned as were the outbuildings. Her father, John Lindley, with whom she and the children were likely living, was shot and killed from ambush while sowing wheat in 1863. The slaves, by whatever means, went free.

Like the Carricos, though, the Mitchells found renewed prosperity after the war though in 1870 the Census reported the value of their land and personal property was about $116,000 in 2021 dollars, some $360,000 less than in 1860. The difference primarily reflects the value of the freed slaves. The Census, of course, lists all the assets as his.

Three of the children who endured the Carrico and Mitchell families' tribulations grew up to play prominent roles in Jerico. Laura Mitchell, 11 years old when the war started, would later marry Dr. Joseph Brasher; Sarah Carrico, 8 years old at war's beginning, married James K, Peer; and Joseph Carrico Jr., six years old when his family was forced out of Cedar County, was later among Jerico's most prominent citizens.

Mildred Hendrick's experience was not unlike those of Eleanor Carrico and Mary Jane Mitchell, though she likely endured fewer of the brutal hardships visited upon them. Seventeen years old when she married 23-year-old school teacher James Cogle in 1861 in Prairie County, Arkansas, she followed her Indiana-born husband north to St. Louis, Mo., when the Civil War began a few weeks later. He joined the Army there and served until the end of the war. Mildred may have been able to see her husband relatively frequently, or even move to where he was, since he was an artillery officer who spent at least part of the war in the forts along the Mississippi River.

After the war, the two went to Cedar County, where over the course of the next 20 years she bore nine children while assisting in his twin careers as farmer and politician/civic leader.

11. Smoking, drinking and dancing

As the 1880s waned, Jerico shed some of the wild and woolly boomtown reputation earned in 1882-83 and was eager to lose more of it. An-anti-alcohol crusade was a key element in the campaign in a town with several saloons. Those included one operated by the firm of Divine & Bible, the *Hermitage Index* noted wryly.

The five churches that had sprung up in Jerico were joined in the anti-booze campaign by a strong local chapter of the Women's Christian Temperance Union and its affiliate for children, the Loyal Temperance Union.

Anti-alcohol gains were hinted at in the Jan. 5, 1888 Stockton Journal, when the paper's Jerico correspondent credited the W.C.T.U. with the fact New Year's Eve had passed without drunken rowdiness in Jerico. The antis hauled out a big gun for the 1890 Jerico Picnic, which had evolved in eight years into a major regional event that drew three to 10 times the town's population, depending primarily on the weather. The crowd in 1890 was described by the *Stockton Journal* only as a "great multitude." The speakers – always a big draw in the pre-radio and television era – would include Jacob Faith, from neighboring Montevallo, a horticulturist known throughout the Midwest. He was equally well-known as an anti-tobacco and alcohol crusader. It was alcohol in his sights this day. The *Stockton Journal* even ran a transcription of his speech.

After praising previous speakers – "I feel that I am like a little canoe floating on the ocean among great steamers." - and the town - "On all our globe there is no grander place to build a sweet home than ... Jerico Springs, a centerpiece of the continent for fruit and health" - Mr. Faith signaled he was ready to get down to business by holding up a glass of water in one hand and a flask of whiskey in the other

"Jerico needs few druggists, and no saloons. Here is a cup of pure medical water which has no equal to relieve sufferers and quench thirst. There is no poison in that cup; to turn you and me and others to ruin. No spectral shadow plays upon the surface of this cup to lower the soul to endless ruin. No orphans' tears rise to God from the placid fountains. Crimes and woe come not where cold water reigns supreme. Pure now as when it left its native heaven brewed by the Almighty and the green glade and grassy dale, giving vigor and health to young and old. It is beautiful and bright in the moonlight fountains and sunny rills. To our lips the cold beautiful water has no equal to quench thirst and is the most relished gift of God's blessings.

"Here is the glass of whiskey, the intoxicating cup. It may be called a poor imitation of the wine that the Almighty made, when he made wine out of water for our use and benefit, if made and used in its place. But I am sorry to say that nowadays most liquors are made from poisonous drugs and a curse to the human family in which peace love hope and truth dwell not within the desolation monster called whiskey. Corrupt now as when it left its native still, giving fire to the eye, madness to the brain and ruin to the soul.

"There is poison in this cup whose sting is madness and embrace is death. There dwells beneath this smiling surface a fiendish spirit which for centuries has been wandering over this Earth carrying on a war of desolation and destruction against mankind, blighting the noble affections of the heart and corrupting with his foul breath the glad green earth. Gaze on but shudder as you gaze. Those sparkling drops are murderers in disguise. Widow's groans and orphan's tears and maniac yells are in this cup. The worm that dieth not and the fire that is never quenched are in this cup.

"It is not in my power to unfold the history of dark records of the past, and point you to the ruined empires and kingdoms that sleep in a cold robbers grave. Intoxicating drinks cause more woe and sorrow and robs more souls of the heavenly kingdom than war and pestilence combined. Young men, let me say to you, bright as is your morning does shine and high as your hopes beat in your bosom, if you be drinking daily, even temporarily, your bright morning will end in clouds and then darkness."

Mr. Faith must have been a hit for he was invited back for the 1891 picnic.

There may have been at least one vote on banning alcohol in Jerico sometime in the 1890s but the record isn't clear. Even if the town did get rid of saloons, drug stores generally stocked whiskey. In 1896, several Jerico druggists were arrested and charged with illegal sale of alcohol. The outcome of the cases is missing.

Another "morality" issue created controversy in 1896 when one church's preacher – which one wasn't reported - attacked dancing in fiery language that offended residents who enjoyed dancing. They responded in a letter to the editor of the *El Dorado Springs Sun:*

Claims to be slandered

"JERICO SPRINGS, MO., Missouri, Jan. 28, 1896 – To the editor of THE SUN: Will you please favor us with a *place in the columns of your paper for this contribution.*

"The object of this is to place before the public the slanderous remarks of censure, insinuations and insults cast by one preacher from the pulpit Sunday night, January 26, at Jerico Springs, Mo., on the young ladies and gentlemen who dance and attend dances. The following are some of the epithets that this slanderer heaped upon the heads of those of that audience that night:

"They who dance are the scum of the earth, that no intelligent or moral people dance," and to further insult the dignity of the gentleman and shock the sensitive feelings of the ladies he said, 'Ladies, when you take the man's hand in the ballroom how do you know that it is not a hand which has just had hold of the hand of a harlot, and that there is not a young man who attends dances that would not seek the downfall of the young ladies attending. 'Might he not as well have said that the young ladies are accomplices of the young men in as much as people are known by the company they keep? Thus did the slanderer heap his tirade of abuse on those of that audience that night.

"We will now ask, by what right did he take the liberty to assault and insult people with this disgraceful language? Was he too ignorant to realize (or too mean to care) the sweeping range of such language as he made to yourself on that night? Are not these young people who dance near and dear to parents, brothers, sisters, relatives and friends everywhere?

"When a man stands in the pulpit and utters these words before a respectable audience, that moral people as a class do not attend dances, that it is the lowest class of people who do attend them, and censures young men with carnal intent with young ladies on such occasions and those young ladies being the associates of young men – we would ask again: Do not such utterances incense the feelings of every parent, relative and friend of these young people? Do they not invade nearly every family circle, penetrating to the very center of the fireside around which the most sacred ties cluster?

"We would ask once more, seriously, is there anyone possessed of a good conscience, who would approve of this slanderer's insults? To the contrary are we not justified in believing that all moral and dignified people will join us in vindicating our rights and reputations and condemning a man who will utter such bitter invectives as being an unprincipled reviler? And, it would seem, who had no other object in view but to try to ruin the reputations of all who dance.

"In conclusion we state that we are a few of the great community at large who dance, but ever stand ready to defend our reputations and rights against the attacks of anyone who will come before the public to slander us and lie on us."

"Jericoans"

12. *Running in place*

Jerico finished second when the 1890 Census rendered its verdict on the three neighboring resort towns founded in 1881-82.

Last was Zodiac Springs, six miles to the west, which never incorporated and wasn't counted as a separate place. There wasn't much there after nine years: a post office, a small hotel and bathhouse, a couple of stores, a handful of houses and no ambition to be more.

Jerico Springs, with 486 permanent residents, played bigger than it was, with its steady stream of visitors to the springs and to a shopping district sized to the needs of several thousand farmers rather than a few hundred townsmen. It was full of men ambitious to further grow their town, which was just 22 people short of matching the population of Stockton, the long-established county seat.

El Dorado Springs, 20 miles to the north, had everything Jerico had and more, including a population of 1,543, three times larger than Jerico's. The explanation was simple: better springs, better roads and more money.

A Report on the Mineral Waters of Missouri, published by the State Geological Survey in December, 1892, enunciates the differences. Based on field and laboratory research conducted during 1890-92, the report contained a geological history of the state, a discussion of the various types of springs and chemical analyses of 83 mineral springs. The otherwise technical report included observations about the resorts around those springs that had one.

The section on El Dorado was three times as long as the one on Jerico and filled with positive words. The "ever-flowing" spring in the park was putting out 180 gallons an hour, and was but one of several springs available. Noted, too, was the "pleasant" two-and a half hour drive to Schell City, the nearest rail station; and the daily stage to Nevada, 20 miles west, "for the most part over good roads." The author estimated $80,000 ($2 million in 2020) had been spent on hotels, bath houses and a casino hall. "Guests and patients are well taken care of and receive the comforts they have a right to expect," the report said.

Of Jerico, it said in its entirety: (emphasis added)

"(The spring) was known and valued by the Indians, who resorted to it long after the country was settled. The water is recommended for rheumatism, kidney and stomach diseases and others. It issues on property belonging to the town but is managed by M. J. Straight, the owner of the bath houses erected near, who is known as the proprietor. *Scant accommodation and difficulty reaching the place retard its development. This is a feebly flowing spring,* a pump being erected to obtain the water supply for the bath houses. Baths are given both hot and cold, the warm baths being recommended. The water is strongly chalybeate and deposits a heavy mass of iron oxide on standing in the cold or on being heated."

Jerico's offerings got a more favorable review about a month later, on Jan. 29, 1893, when *The Springfield Daily Leader's* roaming reporter, "Rambler," published his account of a visit there a few days earlier.

Rambler toured the town in company with – who else - Charley Whitsitt. (One suspects that Mr. Whitsitt arranged the visit in an attempt to counter whatever negative impressions were left by the state report issued a month earlier.) Of the springs, Rambler wrote, "They are beautifully located and this should be one of the most prominent places of resort in Southern Missouri.

"There is to be extensive improvements made on the buildings and grounds this coming spring with a view of accommodating the guests the coming season. There are hot and cold shower baths arranged to suit the most fastidious. Another thing unusual in health resorts is in having first-class hotel accommodations at reasonable rates. Taking this in consideration there is no more pleasant place to be found to spend a few days during the summer months for recreation than this," Rambler wrote.

Writing primarily for a Springfield audience, he said "persons desiring to visit this place during the coming season will take the ... railroad to Lockwood and from there take the United States Mail Stages and enjoy the beautiful scenery on the route."

The Jerico men weren't discouraged by El Dorado's faster growth; if anything, it drove them to greater efforts in their twin searches for railroads and minerals.

The railroad situation essentially was unchanged during Jerico's first eight years. As the 1890s began, the town, indeed all of Cedar County, was surrounded by railroads, the tracks forming the same irregular rectangle that had existed in 1882. It was still 16 miles west to the nearest station, in Sheldon; still 20 miles south to Lockwood; 22 miles southwest to Lamar, now a rail crossroads; and 25 miles southeast to Greenfield, where a spur line from the south ended.

Extending that Greenfield spur through Cedar County and on northward to an eventual connection to Kansas City had considerable support as the new decade arrived. The Greenfield and Northern's chief promoter was T. A. Miller, the South Greenfield businessman who had supplied some of the lumber that built Jerico.

Like all railroad promoters, Mr. Miller wanted financial support from towns along the proposed route, in this case from Greenfield to Arcola to Stockton. On Jan. 2, 1890, Dan Stratton stopped by the office of the *Stockton Journal* to announce he would contribute 40 acres toward the $25,000 bonus ($715,000 in 2020) that was among the incentives Mr. Miller wanted. The *Journal* said Mr. Stratton is "a progressive citizen and never fails to donate something to all public enterprises."

Just more than a year later, in March 1891, the *Journal* announced that "every detail of the contract made between Mr. Miller and the people of Stockton and Arcola have been complied with" and all that remained was for Mr. Miller to do his part. Alas.

Jerico fared no better with its own hot prospect of 1890, the proposed Kansas City, Nevada and Fort Smith. In May, the *Nevada Noticer* said surveyors were reporting that a line that bypassed Jerico well to the west would be 12 miles shorter and cost $12,000 a mile less to build.

In June, the *Springfield Republican* reported that the Santa Fe's purchase of the Frisco System meant the old Kansas City, Monett and Southern proposal was back on the table, with the difference that it would go east from Jerico to Bolivar rather than south to Monett.

In June of 1892, the Kansas City, El Dorado and Southern was chartered. Once built to El Dorado, the road's organizers planned to go on south, perhaps through Jerico, perhaps through Stockton. It got to El Dorado but never beyond.

In Autumn, 1892, when a pair of mining organizations in Springfield planned a meeting to discuss running a railroad to the Dade County coalfields, Charley Whitsitt got wind of it and secured an invitation to bring examples of Cedar County coal and to make a presentation on the advantages of extending the line into Cedar County, too. The project was "heartily" endorsed by the "Mining Bureau and the people of Springfield."

And in December, 1892, the Greenfield and Northern was back with a new proposal. The *Nevada Noticer* said on the 15th that it was "practically settled that the Greenfield and Northern would go to Jerico and El Dorado and Nevada."

The mind-numbing round of proposals and meetings, all faithfully attended by representatives of Jerico who faithfully pledged significant financial support to any road that passed through the town, resulted in nothing, not so much as a mile of actual track. The pace grew less frenetic after 1892, to judge by the greatly reduced volume of newspaper stories about railroads that survive from the remaining years of the decade. A dizzying new round of proposals would arrive with the 20th Century.

The search for minerals seemed ready to pay off as the '90s began.

On July 24, 1890, the *Stockton Journal* carried a *Jerico Optic* story reporting that, "New developments almost daily are being brought to light in the findings of lead and zinc ore." A. M. Heifner, the *Optic* publisher, said "the table in front of me" contained examples of fine zinc ore brought in by M. J. Straight, the bath house operator. The ore was found nine feet down by well-diggers on the George Brasher farm a mile and a half southwest of Jerico. The *Optic* said Jerico's leading mineral experts thought the vein would broaden as it went deeper.

Charley Whitsitt was in on the hunt, too. A month later, the *Optic* reported that he "pulled out Tuesday morning with two of Jerico's mineral experts to locate mineral lands somewhere in Cedar County." Mr. Whitsitt declined to tell the paper where he was going. "Charley does not tell all he knows," the editor noted.

Mr. Straight by 1893 was the central figure in the search for ore, as general manager of the Jerico Mining and Prospecting Company. He had sold his interest in the bath houses to J. M. Black.

The steady stream of hope-inspiring finds continued though none led to major deposits.

13. Moving on education

As the '90s began the Jerico men, acting in cooperation with the Lutherans who ran the college in Jerico, also moved to build a larger role for the town in Cedar County's educational system.

The origins of the college are lost, as is its location in town prior to 1891. The first mention of it comes in the *Stockton Journal's* "Jerico Jottings" column of Jan. 2, 1888, which reported the "college students are returning and there are more of them."

The Lutheran College building in Jerico was co-owned by the Jerico Educational Institute. This photo was taken in 1897, the year after Jerico bought the building for its school.

It is next mentioned in the July 2, 1891, *Journal,* which reported college buildings were going up in El Dorado and Jerico," and on July 23, the *Journal* reported that Dan Stratton's "College Addition to the town of Jerico Springs has been filed for the record. The people of Jerico Springs will make the college a success."

The effort to make it a success included the creation of the Jerico Educational Institute. Incorporation papers were filed by Dr. Brasher in early July. He was president of the five-member board of managers, which included Charley Whitsitt and his real estate business partner C. S. Brown. Dr. Brasher's younger brother, Byron, now cashier at the Hartley bank, was the treasurer.

The Jerico Educational Institute and the Lutherans (probably in the legal form of the Kansas Synod) jointly owned the building that was going up on what thereafter was known as College Hill.

The JEI arranged training programs for teachers in which the college's three-person faculty conducted classes. The "teachers' institutes" were four- to six-week sessions in the summer that provided both continuing education and preparatory training for Missouri state teacher certification tests. Held previously at various places around the county, the institutes became a fixture in Jerico in the early 1890s.

The "Teachers Training School" for 1893, for example, was a six-week affair that included courses in "School Management, Methods of Teaching, Psychology Applied in Teaching, History of Education and a Study of the Lives of Eminent Teachers."

The county teachers' organization paid the 50 to 125 people who attended $2 a week ($63 in 2021) to help defray expenses. The resulting influx of money and people temporarily added 10-25 percent to the town's population, filling hotels and private homes and bringing on a lively social season.

The collaboration between the Lutherans and the JEI may have led to a short-lived plan to build a major Lutheran community near Jerico. Stories in several newspapers around Missouri and Kansas in 1894 said, in sum, that the Lutherans planned to buy 2,700 acres near Jerico and establish a community that would include a $75,000 college campus ($2.3 million in 2020). The plan died because Lutheran Church authorities decided Jerico was too far from a railroad, according to the Rev. J. A. Lowe, a key figure in the transfer of the college/JEI building to the village of Jerico in 1896.

That transfer occurred when the Lutherans apparently gave up on the college just when Jerico was looking for a new school building. Voters in September of 1895 approved the issuance of $1,000 in bonds ($31,000 in 2020) to "purchase the Jerico college building and use the same for public school purposes," the El Dorado Sun reported. The college building served as Jerico's schoolhouse until 1914, when it was replaced by the brick building that served as long as Jerico had a school.

The teachers' institutes continued to be held in Jerico for a few years, and then in rotation with other towns for a period before they were discontinued.

14. The Hartley bank fails

Eighteen ninety-three brought the Jerico men their first major setback. In late June, the nine-year-old Hartley Bank failed, with the loss ultimately passing $30,000 ($850,000 in 2020).

The bank's cashier, Byron Brasher, Dr. Brasher's younger brother, made the failure into a sensation when he set fire to the bank in the wee morning hours of June 28, 1893, then told townsmen rushing to the scene that armed men had taken him from his home to the bank and set the fire in frustration when their robbery attempt was foiled by a time lock on the safe.

B. L. Brasher, his wife Sidney and one of their children. He bore the brunt of the blame for the 1893 failure of the Hartley Bank of Jerico, where he was cashier.

His story soon fell apart and his now former friends, caught in the fever of the moment, talked of hanging him but when they went to his house to arrest him, he held them at bay with a pistol while he fled. Calmer heads soon prevailed and Jerico got on with assessing the damage and repairing it.

Creditors named C. S. Brown, Mr. Whitsitt's real estate partner, as assignee to assess claims against the bank, with an advisory committee comprising Charles Sheppard, Crafton Beydler, and Judge J. F. Brown, according to the *Jerico Advocate*, a short-lived competitor of the *Optic*. The story also said, "Suits were immediately brought against the officers of the bank and attachment served on the entire real property of A. M. Pyle, president; Joseph Carrico, Sr., vice president; B. L. Brasher, cashier; also Dr. J. P. Brasher and Frank Brasher, directors."

The *Dade County Advocate*'s summary of the situation in its July 6 issue, a week later, proved largely accurate.

> "Brother Brackett of the Jerico Advocate called on us last Monday, and tells us that excitement in his city over the recent bank robbery there was very high. It seems to be the prevailing opinion there that the job was put up by cashier Brasher and no actual robbery occurred. The bank has gone into the hands of a receiver.

> "This makes things bad for the Jerico people as the bank was a popular one and many of the merchants and businessmen in the town kept their money there and had accumulated deposits there to beat bills coming due. Many stockmen, too, who are now or were buying for feeding for the fall markets had their deposits in this bank, and the wreck has been a paralyzer of business.

> "Depositors are wild with suspense and excitement and strong talk of violence to the cashier has been indulged in, so much so the cashier refuses to give himself into the hands of the Jerico authorities, but we understand is willing to surrender to the authorities of Stockton.

> "The affair is a very unfortunate one as it is likely that the affairs and money of the bank will be tied up in the courts and estate business for some time. It seems to us that the depositors ought to suffer no other loss, however, than the delay and any inconvenience, as the bank is a private one and the partnership well worth the total of the liabilities, as we understand it.

> "The latest rumors we get from Jerico are to the effect that it is believed that neither depositors nor stockholders will lose anything. The cash in the bank and collateral and other securities will when finally wound up make everyone interested whole."

The last paragraph was inaccurate in details, as it turned out. The assets of the bank proved insufficient to cover the losses, with depositors getting back just 20 cents on the dollar. The balance was in the end covered by Dr. Brasher, three of his brothers and a cousin, who together held a controlling interest in the bank. On March 10, 1894, the *Springfield Democrat* reported the assignee handling the bank's affairs "is now advertising for sale those pieces of property turned over by the Brashers to make the loss good."

Though it's not necessarily an accurate measure of what they gave up, the five Brashers holding controlling interest in the bank had a total of 940 acres around the future site of Jerico in 1879, according to a plat map from that year. Their holdings were reduced to 291 acres by 1897 after the bank's affairs had been settled, according to a plat map from that year.

At least one business was caught in the undertow and failed. J. W. C. Brown, formerly the partner of James Peer, had just borrowed money from the Hartley bank to buy his own hardware store "and the recent bank failure, together with slow collections" forced it to close its doors, the *Jerico Advocate* reported.

An exact cause for the failure apparently was never established. The Panic of 1893 was touching Cedar County, according to the *Republican*, which said a couple of weeks after the closure that farmers were "financially strapped" and all classes were suffering as a result. The newspapers, though, never mentioned the panic as a factor in the bank's problems. Byron Brasher was charged with accepting deposits into a bank he knew was failing but those counts were later dismissed in favor of a larceny charge. He was found not guilty in January, 1896, by a jury in Barton County, where the trial was held on a change of venue.

Charley Whitsitt and Joseph Morris didn't wait for all that to play out. Acting in concert to restore movement to Jerico's "paralyzed" business community, they formed the Morris Banking Co., with Mr. Morris as president and Mr. Whitsitt as cashier. The venture was announced in October, barely three months after the Hartley failure. Capital stock was $5,000 ($145,000 in 2020).

The Morris Bank never opened. An outside investor, Peter Lloyd of Mount Ida, Ia., appeared on the scene and The P. Lloyd Bank "superseded" the Morris bank in November, 1893. How Mr. Lloyd came to know of Jerico and why he chose to invest there are lost to history but he brought money to the table: The new bank had $20,000 in capital ($578,000 in 2020). Mr. Whitsitt was cashier; Charles Sheppard, Joe Carrico Jr.'s business partner, was vice president, and would later be replaced by Mr. Carrico. All but Mr. Lloyd were Jerico residents but whatever per centage of the bank they owned, Mr. Lloyd held controlling interest.

15. The tornado of 1898

Sunday, May, 1, 1898, was a sultry Spring day in Jerico, the morning air carrying hints of a looming storm. Mrs. George Clark had other things on her mind as she left the Methodist Church before services ended and returned to her home directly across the street to the south. It was her 35th birthday and she was busy "preparing something extra" for the noon-time meal when a tornado spawned by the storm struck.

It destroyed the Clark home, killing Mrs. Clark and severely injuring her husband, leveled the church while it was still filled with worshippers and took the roof off the Neumann House hotel before skipping out of town. Miraculously, no one was killed in the church though the *Cedar County Republican* listed the names of six people with broken bones and said "many others had cuts and bruises, or were injured getting out of the building."

Mollie Gates, the wife of Dr. Lester Gates was among the dozens of people filling the church. In a letter written to her sister in Oklahoma two weeks later, she described the horror that descended upon the church that day.

"It got cloudy while we were at Sunday School. We came near coming home after Sunday School, but concluded we would stay for preaching. While we were singing the first song it got so dark we could scarcely see the words in the book, and it began to rain furiously. I just thought it was going to be a hard rain and maybe hail, but did not think of a cyclone.

"After the song, the preacher prayed, and just as he said Amen, the window shutters slammed shut on the south side of the house and on

The Methodist Church in Jerico was full of worshipers when a tornado brought it down May 1, 1898. Miraculously, no one was killed in the church though Mrs. George Clark was killed in her house across the street when it, too, was destroyed.

the north side too, and the windows on both sides seemed to bend inward, and the timbers began to pop and everybody jumped up to get out, and before they could leave their seats, the building went down.

"The last thing I remember was hearing the house pop, and then I felt the floor move like a boat, and I felt nothing else till I was being pulled out. I did not feel myself fall or feel anything strike me. When I came to myself, I was lying on my left side and could not see a bit of light anywhere. I managed to turn over on my elbows and then I saw light in the west, and I tried to crawl out but I couldn't. The roof was so close to me I could not raise up only on my elbows. Frank Davis pulled me out. If you could see the ruins, you would wonder that we all got out alive. All that were injured are getting well.

"You know the church faced the east. I was sitting in the choir in the northwest corner of the church, with my back to the north. The building moved about twenty feet off the foundation before it fell.

"The north side fell to the north. The west end was blown out and turned clear over with the weather boarding up. The south side came down on the south half of the floor and the roof fell with the south edge about middle way off the floor and the north edge on the north wall. The chairs held the south wall and the roof off of the people.

"I did not say a word till I got out. Then I began to cry and scream for Lester (her husband). He was away out southwest of town, and I was scared to death until he came home. It seems the wind just came down right at Mr. (George) Clark's house (where it killed Mrs. Clark), and we can see the path of it from there to the church, then it raised and struck the Neumann Hotel at the second story.

"The church was insured for $700 ($22,300 in 2021) and the contents for two hundred dollars ($6,400 in 2021). They have paid it already and we will commence building soon," Mrs. Gates said.

The church was rebuilt within months. The Clark house wasn't, and its loss destroyed a link to Jerico's earliest days – it was the house moved from Charley Whitsitt's farm to become Jerico's first building, used as a hotel and then as the town's first school before being turned to use as a house again.

The Neumann House was repaired and served for an additional 10 years before being torn down in 1908.

16. The thinning

The 1890s removed five of Jerico's eight core founders, three by death and two by retirement.

The first to go was Morris Mitchell, who was two weeks short of 72 when he died June 17, 1893. The *Kansas City Star's* short obituary said he had fought in "every major Civil War battle west of the Mississippi." Throw in service in the Mexican War in the 1840s and a trip to the California goldfields and a term as Cedar County sheriff in the 1850s, and Mr. Mitchell's life had been a continuous adventure story.

✳His descendants founded and ran Mitchell's Hardware store in Jerico until 1950 or so.✳

Next was Joe Carrico Sr., who died Aug. 6, 1898, at age 79. The *Stockton Journal* said he was "genial, jovial, and but few men had keener sense

J. B. Carrico Sr.

of wit and humor. He was always ready with something to provoke a smile without a sting.

"As a public speaker he was ready and argumentative – springing quaint and effective illustrations.

"Had Mr. Carrico received a thorough collegiate education some of his marked, attractive and distinctive individuality might have been suppressed, but it would not have made him a better man," the Journal said.

The deaths of Mr. Mitchell and Mr. Carrico were hardly surprising, given their age, but that of Dr. J. P. Brasher shocked Jerico and Cedar County. Just 49 when he died Sept. 2, 1899, Dr. Brasher had continued in public life after the disaster that befell his family when the Hartley Bank collapsed. He had chaired the Democrats' county convention in 1898 and was a delegate to the senatorial convention the same year.

The funeral of Dr. Joseph Brasher drew a huge crowd of mourners to the Methodist Church in Jerico Sept. 3, 1899. (Ancestry.com)

The circumstances of his death were unusual – the *El Dorado Springs Sun* said they "beget a suspicion of suicide." The doctor had been called to visit a patient on Friday, Sept. 1 and didn't return home. He was found the next morning a mile and a half west of Jerico, his horse tied to a tree and him lying unconscious on the ground with the cushion from the buggy and his coat for bedding. Taken home, he was treated by Jerico's three other doctors to no avail and died Saturday evening.

The *Sun* said he had stopped at a house on the way home, asked for a cup of coffee and while drinking it said he wasn't feeling well and took a dose of medicine, supposedly morphine, before leaving. He had gone but a short distance when he tied the horse and lay down. The funeral, held Sunday afternoon some 18 hours after he died, drew a huge crowd to the Methodist church in Jerico.

Daniel Stratton and James Cogle were alive, but no longer factors in Jerico's civic affairs.

Mr. Stratton, in ill health for several years, was "quite feeble," the *Optic* reported Feb. 17, 1898. It said, "His mind has again become affected and his condition makes it possible that his days of usefulness are over. He has the sympathy of the entire community."

He and Emily moved to Colorado Springs, Col., where they lived with their daughter, Minnie Morrison. Mr. Stratton listed his profession as "gold miner" on the 1900 Census. Emily died Aug. 26, 1900. He died four months later, Dec. 20, 1900. The local paper, in a one paragraph obituary, said he died "after a long illness. The deceased had been suffering from brain trouble for some time."

Mr. Whitsitt, had been trying to sell Mr. Stratton's Cedar County holdings since 1898 – a 1900 advertisement in the Cedar County Republican said "Daniel Stratton's lands in Cedar County are being sold cheap for cash. Contact C. E. Whitsitt" - but there was considerable remaining when he died without a will. His heirs, who had all scattered, asked Mr. Whitsitt to continue but it was years before Mr. Stratton's affairs were settled.

Whatever success Mr. Cogle enjoyed in Jerico's first years, had faded by 1890 when his large two-story brick building at the northeast corner of Broadway and Main was sold at a sheriff's sale to satisfy an unpaid note which Mr. Cogle had secured with the building.

He rebounded and in 1893 was running a feed store, as opposed to his earlier general merchandise stores. By 1900, though, he was 66 and retired. He lived until 1912, when the *Optic* said in his obituary, in addition to recounting the fact he'd been Jerico's first merchant, "During the early history of our city, he was a power in politics and was a leader of the Republican party."

The 1890s overall saw Jerico running in place, in the most favorable view. The 1900 Census showed the population had fallen by 8 per cent, to 443, even as the county's had increased by 8 per cent, Stockton's by

9.3 per cent and El Dorado's by 29 per cent. The railroad map was unchanged, with the exception that a spur line had been extended into El Dorado from the northwest, but it was of no utility to Jerico.

Jerico nevertheless remained a lively place. It continued to play bigger than it was. It still had its dreams. It still had men willing to pursue them. If death had caught up with some of its early leaders, new men had emerged to join Charley Whitsitt, Joe Carrico Jr. and James Peer as civic leaders in the new century.

Among them Francis M. Bruster and E. R. Hightower, both lawyers, real estate promoters, insurance agents and loan brokers who advertised Jerico's attributes throughout Missouri and beyond. Each played various roles in the efforts to bring a railroad to town.

Dr. Lester Gates and William T. Neal, a future dentist, were each taking on bigger roles in Jerico and in its dealings with its neighbors. So were J. W. Jones, a newcomer from Nebraska who also was in the real estate game and R. C. Laing, a building contractor and long-time Jerico resident.

17. Confronting time and tide

The year 1900 began, as had each of Jerico's years, with the never-ending searches for mineral wealth and railroads.

Mr. Straight and the Jerico Mining and Prospecting Co. were gone, replaced in 1900 by the Carrico Mining Co., founded by J. B. Carrico. Joining him in the venture were his sometimes business partner C. W. Sheppard, real estate agent J. W. Jones and banker Peter Lloyd. There were exploratory shafts going down at unspecified sites in Cedar and Dade counties in hopes of finding paying quantities of lead and/or zinc.

On April 19, the *Cedar County Republican* reported "that Jerico prospectors have struck 16 feet of jack (a desirable variation of zinc ore) at the Sharp mine near Cedar Creek at a depth of 200 feet. The drill has been stopped and the shaft will be put down at once." The story didn't say whether the prospectors were from Mr. Carrico's new company.

There were at least two mining operations at work in the area southeast of Jerico in the summer of 1900 when the *Optic's* A. M, Heifner visited, along with a correspondent from a Nevada paper. One was at the farm of A. M. Pyle, the cattleman who had served as president of the Hartley Bank. Mr. Heifner reported a "rich vein" had been discovered and that Mr. Pyle had three shafts working, one down 120 feet, one down 185 feet and the third, 215 feet. He said the hole being drilled at the moment was showing the highest percent of ore (what ore was unspecified).

On the way back to Jerico Mr. Heifner, without specifying where, "visited the Carrico Mining Company's shaft," where he was told a night shift would soon be added to drive ahead "as fast as possible."

Like all other lead and zinc mining ventures around Jerico, those underway in 1900 came to nothing in the end despite tempting finds.

A 1901 ad in the Jerico Springs Optic for J. B. Carrico's Little Acorn Department Store. The store, which in 1904 had nearly $500,000 in annual sales in 2021 dollars, was probably Jerico's second largest retailer behind Peer Hardware.

The Carrico Mining Company investment was the last made in Jerico by Peter Lloyd, president of the P. Lloyd Banking Co. He died Aug. 16, 1901, with his death touching off of a competition for control of Jerico's banking business.

Richard Jones, Mr. Lloyd's nephew who had moved to Jerico when the bank was founded in 1893, was chosen to succeed Mr. Lloyd as bank president. Mr. Whitsitt, who had worked to bring Mr. Lloyd to Jerico in 1893, resigned as cashier and announced he was organizing the Bank of Jerico.

The new bank opened Oct. 18, 1901 after selling $12,000 in capital stock ($370,000 in 2021), the *Optic* reported. J. W. Nebelsick, a furniture dealer/undertaker, was president and Mr. Whitsitt was cashier. The dozen stockholders included Mr. Whitsitt's longtime ally Joseph Morris and two women, Laura Martin and Elizabeth Spencer.

Mr. Jones, upon taking over the Lloyd Bank, created a stir by demanding more security on some loans. The *Optic* said he was shown to be right on that point but Mr. Jones announced less than a year later he was closing out the bank's affairs and pulling out. The *Optic* said he decided the return on capital was insufficient and "after due consideration (he) concluded to close up (the) banking business here with a view of finding a more favorable locality."

The Optic editor was effusive in his praise of Mr. Jones' conduct in wrapping up the bank's business affairs. "Mr. Jones is a gentleman in every particular both socially and morally and has made many friends among Jerico's conservative businessmen and farmers and the P. Lloyd Bank will be missed in our town." That aside, Jerico's bank was once again controlled by Jerico.

The principal railroad proposal floating around as the 20th Century began was the Oklahoma, Central and St. Louis, promoted by a man named W. S. McCaull. It revived the old plan to connect to the extensive Rock Island Lines system at Eldon, south of Jefferson City, and link to Indian Territory (future Oklahoma), this time with the line running through Jerico, Carthage and Joplin.

Mr. McCaull, like most railroad promoters, essentially assembled packages comprising surveys, right-of-way for the road and pledges from towns along the route to supply depots and cash bonuses. With those in hand the promoter turned to big money men for the capital to build and equip the line. It was a system with many fail points, as the Jerico men knew all too well even as they played it again.

On Dec. 18, 1902, the *Kansas City Daily World* reported Mr. McCaull had conducted several railroad-related meetings in that city, including one with J. B. Carrico, president of the Jerico Business Men's Association, and F. M. Bruster, secretary of the town's railroad committee. Topics included depot and terminal arrangements for Jerico, as well as construction of a large new hotel and bath house, the paper said.

Additionally, Mr. McCaull announced to the *Daily World* that a former U. S. attorney for Guthrie, Okla., had been added to the railroad's board of directors and was en route to Washington to handle negotiations with the Department of Interior over right-of-way through the Osage and Cherokee reservations in Indian Territory.

As 1903 began, Jerico's neighbor Golden City enthusiastically joined the list of towns endorsing the effort. At an initial informational meeting, residents pledged 15 miles of right-of-way, grounds for a depot and a cash bonus, hundreds of dollars of which was collected on the spot.

The *Optic* reported Jan. 9, 1903, that the railroad contract discussed in Kansas City had arrived but when the railroad committee met, it rejected the contract because it bound Jerico to deliver the $10,000 bonus ($300,000 in 2021) in cash rather than pledges to be collected by the railroad.   Mr. Bruster was dispatched to Kansas City to renegotiate so that the railroad would do the collecting. Mr. McCaull agreed to the terms requested.

A further sign he was serious about a road through the Jerico coal fields came a week later when he incorporated The Great Northern Fuel Company, the purpose of which was to buy, sell and transport coal.

The Jerico men, apparently eager to see progress and pestering Mr. McCaull, drew a gentle rebuke in March 1903 when the promoter reminded them they had taken seven months to negotiate terms and ought be patient while he completed agreements with 100-plus other towns on the route.

He fell short. The *Sheldon Enterprise* reported June 16, 1903 that Mr. McCaull's proposed road had been dealt "the hatchet blow" by the news that his longstanding claims aside, not all the right of way, particularly that promised by Golden City, had actually been obtained.

Jerico, for its part, had stood ready to meet its obligations, including several miles of right of way, grounds for a station and a $10,000 bonus ($300,000 in 2021) when the tracks reached town.

Charley Whitsitt's first reaction when he received the bad news was to convene a meeting with Sheldon businessmen to discuss construction of an electric rail line between the two towns, an idea that surfaced several times over the years. The *Enterprise* said the Sheldon men were enthusiastic but the idea again went nowhere.

18. 1904: Time of crisis

As 1904 began Jerico faced what would prove to be the most critical 18 months in its history.

With the McCaull railroad proposal definitively dead, the Jerico men, with Charley Whitsitt in the forefront, were forging a railroad plan to replace it that relied upon themselves to the greatest degree ever. It was a bootstrap plan, even a desperate one. Audacious in conception and bold in execution, its success depended – as did all railroad schemes – on a lot of moving pieces fitting together at the right times.

Even as the Jerico men were fitting the first pieces, an unrelated development sowed dissension and discord in their ranks.

In February 1904, J. B. Carrico Jr., and Preston Peer, the son and now-business partner of James K. Peer in Peer & Son Hardware, said they were planning to build a large new building adjacent to Mr. Carrico's Little Acorn department store and combine operations there as the Jerico Mercantile Co.

The Peer hardware operation almost certainly was the town's biggest retailer by dollar volume and among the larger in the region. Mr. Carrico's department store was probably the next largest retailer in Jerico - both he and his wife, Malissa, made regular buying trips to Kansas City and St. Louis and offered a selection of higher-end goods as well as less expensive lines. The new company, said Mr. Carrico and young Mr. Peer, would sell certificates for $10 ($300 in 2021) that were good for a year and would entitle the holder to buy all merchandise for railhead cost plus carriage to Jerico.

Jerico's merchant community exploded in opposition, not to the merger but to the certificate plan. At a public meeting called after word of the plan got out and attended by virtually all the town's businessmen, opponents argued that the certificate system would

Peer Hardware carried an enormous stock.

benefit large customers to the point all other merchants would be driven out of business and a monopoly established. A "conciliating spirit on the part of the Mercantile Company brought things around," and the entire plan was dropped, the *Optic* reported in its March 18, 1904 issue.

It is well the dispute was smoothed over for the Jerico men would soon need every hand pulling together.

On April 29, 1904, the *Jerico Springs Optic* carried three railroad stories. There was a short one informing those who had pledged money toward the McCaull project they could pick up their pledges at the Bank of Jerico, and a long one by *Optic* owner and editor A. M. Heifner in which he restated the benefits to accrue to both Jerico and any railroad that served it. The third story reported on a pair of public meetings that introduced the new railroad plan and the new players.

The men to whom Jerico turned were J. C. Long, a railroad promoter and civil engineer from Little Rock, Ark., and W. S. Allison, a businessman and railroad promoter from El Dorado who had helped bring a spur line into that town from the northwest during the 1890s.

The plan outlined called for the Jerico men to charter their own railroad company and finance a 20-mile track from Jerico to a point near Lamar on one of the two lines that crossed there. Mr. Long and Mr. Allison would see to the surveys required and arrange construction, all the while looking to expand the project to other towns and more investors - they envisioned ultimately making that connection between Eldon and Indian Territory. Jerico would provide a $10,000 bonus ($300,000 in 2021), pay for the survey, a station in Jerico and right of way through Cedar County and portions of Dade and Barton counties.

Little time was thereafter wasted.

May 6, 1904: The *Optic* reported the railroad committee – C. E. Whitsitt, J. B. Carrico, his brother the Rev. W. B. Carrico, Henry Arnold,

W. T. Martin, F. M. Bruster, F. W. Kohlmeier, J. W. Jones, C. W. Brownlee and A. M. Heifner -- had raised $445 ($13,000 in 2021) to buy surveying equipment. Mr. Whitsitt, Mr. Long and Mr. Allison had departed for Kansas City, Mr. Whitsitt on banking business and the two others to buy the surveying tools and related accoutrements.

May 13, 1904: The men and the surveying equipment were back in Jerico, the *Optic* said. Mr. Long and Mr. Allison, aided by a group from the town, had begun the survey. That scene, surely planned with its symbolism in mind, hits with gut-wrenching poignancy when envisioned a century and a quarter later: The surveyors' assistants chosen were the sons of some of Jerico's leading figures. Some were boys, some of them young men, all out assisting in the last-ditch effort to make their fathers' dreams come true. They included Charley Whitsitt's son Ben; J. K. Peer's son J. K. Jr.; Francis Bruster's son Charley; E. R. Hightower's son Howard; A. M. Heifner's son Ern; and W.R. Lakey, son of one of Jerico's earliest merchants.

May 27, 1904: Charley Whitsitt, in a letter to "brother Heifner's good newspaper," declared, "A road means everything to us."

With both frustration and optimism that remain clear more than a century later, he wrote, "We have tried faithfully for the past 20 years to induce some railroad company to put a road through here and no road yet. In fact, we all know that the railroads now surrounding us do not intend to put a road through here, nor do they intend to allow anyone else to do so, and for us to get a road means that we must take hold with some construction company outsiders and induce them to build in here by our assisting them, and by the way of donations, and free right of way and in this way and this alone, I apprehend is the way we will get a road."

He appealed for support for the new project from town and country – a donation of $1 per acre of farm land would bring rich returns in land value once the road was built, he said. Appealing to farmers was a key point, for they, as always, were the real power in Jerico – Mr. Whitsitt and Mr. Bruster once committed to support a railroad proposal only "after checking with our leading farmers."

The failure of earlier projects was no reason to give up, Mr. Whitsitt said in his letter. "Yes, we have so far always failed, and now we lay down just like a sheep surrendered. What?

"No, never. To the earnest and tireless workers, victory is sure. When a community get it all over in earnest concerning any enterprise they must and will succeed. If not at first, sure to later on, as a persistent effort, by an individual or individuals, always comes out on top. It's the steady drop that wears the hole in the rock, and if we continue to work for a road, it is sure we will succeed.

"I am glad I cannot be discouraged in any prize like this. I know we need the road, and I know we can get the road if we as a community will continue to strive for a road. Now let's all sign up for what we might ought to give. Don't try how little you can get off for, but come up like men and do our duty in this time when our help is needed. You will feel better after having done your duty, and each one of us will know about what our part is in such a matter and enterprise as this," he said.

May 28, 1904: Town leaders, at a public meeting held in the park, urged support for the railroad. Speakers included the Rev. W. B. Carrico, brother to Joe Carrico Jr. The *Optic* said that "as he warmed to his subject, he became intensely eloquent." He was followed by C. E. Whitsitt who, the *Optic* said, "grew quite eloquent as he proceeded, dropping hot shot into the camp with every sentence."

The following call for donations "met with some success but not as much as should have been, we think," the *Optic* said. The feeling, however, was "strongly in favor of the railroad."

June 1, 1904: The Jerico and Southwestern Railroad was chartered by the state of Missouri to run 20 miles from Jerico southwest to connect to either the MoPac or Frisco near Lamar. That the exact connect point was still unknown testifies to the ad hoc nature of the effort. Charley Whitsitt was the company's president; J. B. Carrico the vice president; other directors were J. W. Jones, a real estate man; and A. M. Heifner, the newspaper publisher. F. M. Bruster was its attorney.

19. Fire, fire and more fire

Whatever celebratory mood was created by the railroad charter disappeared less than a week later when the greatest disaster in Jerico's history struck. A pair of fires, one in the early morning hours of Saturday, June 4, and the second some 36 hours later, around midnight Sunday, June 5, destroyed Jerico's two largest business buildings along with the inventories of the five major businesses and several smaller ones inhabiting them.

In the single greatest disaster in Jerico's history everything in this picture except the livery stable at center was destroyed by fire June 4-5, 1904 Losses after insurance payments totaled more than $500,000 in 2021 dollars.

The Saturday morning fire hit the two-story brick building at the southwest corner of Main and Broadway built by Charley Whitsitt and Joseph Morris shortly after Jerico was founded and which remained a bustling center of activity.

The east half of the building, now owned by Dr. Lester Gates, housed the Carender and Gates Drug Store on the first floor. The second floor included the medical offices of Dr. Gates and his partner, Dr. Allen; and the law office of E. R. Hightower. The west half, owned by Lew Arnold, was home to Arnold Brothers, a general merchandise and grocery store operated by his brother John, with second floor occupants including a millinery shop owned by a Mrs. Vanhorn and the Woodmen of the World Hall.

A considerable portion of the Arnold Brothers' stock was saved and moved across Main Street into a vacant storefront in the Pickett Block. Otherwise, the building and its contents were a total loss.

There had been a storm around the time of the fire and the initial assumption was that lightning had run in on telephone lines, as had happened a year earlier in the daytime, injuring two people and starting a quickly extinguished fire. That theory disappeared Sunday night when fire struck again, starting in the vacant storeroom in the Pickett building where the Arnolds' goods had been taken.

Built by E. D. Pickett in 1887-88, the Pickett Block was Jerico's largest building, stretching for more than a half block along Main Street beginning at Broadway and running south. The brick structure had four store fronts and a second-floor hall. Mr. Pickett had originally operated a furniture business in one of the storefronts but had moved on and the building was rented out.

R. S. Holman's drug store had the corner store at Broadway; next on the south was James K. Peer's hardware store, now operated in partnership with his son Preston; William Finch, a grocer and dry goods merchant, had the third store and the fourth was vacant. All but Mr. Holman's drug store were destroyed and it was heavily damaged.

Frustratingly for the historian, the *Optic* for June 10, 1904, which would have carried the fire story, is missing from the microfilm record. A half dozen or so accounts from other newspapers do survive. These stories do not say why but there seemed no doubt the second fire was arson and it was soon assumed the first had been as well. The *Lockwood Luminary* reported an attempt had been made to start a third fire on Monday night but alert and nervous townsmen spotted the "incendiary" and fired several shots at him as he fled on horseback.

Either fire would have been a heavy blow; together they were staggering to Jerico. The fact they had been deliberately set would have added an enormous level of concern and worry. The next week's *Henry County Democrat* in Clinton shared the view of a traveling salesman who had passed through Jerico after the fire: "Everybody is discouraged and blue down there. The fire wiped out five of the six good business buildings completely. Unless the town gets the railroad it is hoping for, it is doubtful it will be rebuilt."

The salesman underestimated both the number of good business buildings in Jerico and the determined spirit with which it reacted to the disaster. Disaster it *had* been. The loss in the Pickett building fire was estimated at $30,000 ($875,000 in 2021), with insurance covering about 50 per cent, according to the newspaper stories. In the Gates-Arnold building fire, the owners and tenants incurred a combined loss in excess of $10,000 ($290,000 in 2021) with, again, about half covered by insurance.

Even after the insurance, then, Jerico's merchants incurred a loss of more than $500,000 in 2021 dollars. Hardly helpful to the fund-raising for the railroad project, or anything else.

Multi-building and multi-block downtown fires in places big and small were common – and sometimes town-killing. El Dorado and Stockton were among the places that fought back after major fires. With its first official action following the devastating weekend blazes, Jerico signaled its intent to join the survivors: The annual Founders Day picnic, scheduled for June 9, the Thursday following the fires, would go on.

Some of the scheduled attractions had to be canceled. But the crowd gathered in the park, a quarter of which was bordered by newly burned-out buildings, "was a big one" that enjoyed a drill team performance, speeches by political candidates and conversations with friends, the *Optic* said. The day closed with an evening concert "that was most charming, and great credit is due our boys for the sweet melodies that rolled out on the evening breeze and was lost in the echoes of the distant hills and vales."

As those echoes faded away, Jerico's leaders turned to face the enormous tasks before them. Dr. Gates almost immediately vowed to replace his building, but for several months the recovery news was about relocating some of the burned-out businesses, or ads from businessmen asking for repayment of all outstanding debt. "I am needing the money very badly," John Arnold declared in his ad.

20. The railroad comes first

Fire recovery, though, apparently took a back seat to the railroad project, which moved ahead rapidly as befitted work that "is everything to us," in Mr. Whitsitt's words.

June 24, 1904: Less than three weeks after the fires, Mr. Whitsitt and the other railroad officers met with Mr. Long and Mr. Allison in Mr. Bruster's office and went paragraph by paragraph over the contract to build the road. The pact was approved and – in another testament to the ad hoc nature of the effort - the group set out for Lamar to drum up support for the project there.

The Jerico men called ahead to arrange a 7:30 p.m. meeting at the Pickwick Hotel and arrived to find the lobby packed by interested Lamar citizens, including many businessmen. Mr. Bruster, Mr. Whitsitt and Mr. Long made short speeches outlining the project, after which the Lamar people "became enthused and at once set about to elect committees to carry out their part of the work, which is to get right of way to Horse Creek, the *Optic* said."

July, 8, 1904: Mr. Long and Mr. Allison visited Jerico, reported arrangements were progressing well and said it was time for Jerico to get its bonus ready because the money would soon be necessary.

July 11-12, 1904: A. M. Heifner, the *Optic* editor and a director of the railroad company, spent two days securing pledges for the right-of-way needed through Cedar and Dade counties, as well as that needed in Barton County from the Dade County line to Horse Creek.

August 8, 1904: The *Optic* reprinted stories from The Cedar County Republican and Humansville Star Leader reporting that Mr. Long has been touring a possible extension for the Jerico and Southwestern into the Jefferson City area.

September, 23, 1904: The Jefferson City, Jerico and Southwestern Railroad is chartered by Mr. Long and Mr. Allison with $1.25 million in capital stock ($36.7 million in 2021). The stockholders were Judus R. Long of Little Rock (probably a relative of J. C. Long), Mr. Allison and three St. Louis investors. The charter authorized 125 miles of track from that Rock Island Lines link at Eldon south of Jefferson City to Minden west of Lamar. J. C. Long was a vice president in the new company.

Oct. 7, 1904: The Jerico men, in company with Mr. Long, travel to Lamar to make plain to the people there that it is "time to shoot, or give up the gun." Lamar residents reacted with renewed enthusiasm for the project and huddled with Mr. Long for precise instructions on what right-of-way was needed.

Oct. 14, 1904: Mr. Long and Mr. Allison visit Lamar in company with J. A. Ware, a railroad construction contractor preparing a bid to build the railroad. The trio traveled to Jerico, touring the proposed route as they made the trip.

Nov. 4, 1904: *The Lamar Leader* reports crews working under Mr. Ware have completed the route survey to Horse Creek and that one of the St. Louis investors toured the route.

Nov. 30, 1904: Another fire disaster was narrowly averted when passers-by spotted a fire in the Hayden building on Broadway in time to sound an alarm and save the structure from serious harm. The building, which housed a dry goods store operated by a Mr. Walker, incurred $90 damage ($2,600 in 2021). There was no insurance and the fire's origin was undetermined.

Dec. 30, 1904: In its last issue of eventful 1904, the *Optic* noted in a short story there had been a holiday lull in railroad developments. Nothing had been heard from Mr. Long for a week, Editor Heifner said somewhat snittily.

He wouldn't be disappointed long. As 1905 dawned, the flow of railroad news became a flood that was joined by a steady stream of rebuilding news. Focused though they were on the railroad, Jerico's leaders had been spending some time planning the renewal of their fire-ravaged town.

Jan. 6, 1905: The board of directors of the Bank of Jerico voted at their annual meeting to erect a "commodious" new building come spring, "railroad or no railroad." The structure would be "more portentous" if a railroad was built than if not. In any case, it would be built, bank cashier Charley Whitsitt told the paper.

Jan. 13, 1905: The *Optic* reported Mr. Long had been in town for several days though ill in his room at the Central Hotel under the care of Dr. Gates for most of that time. He told the *Optic* construction crews would soon begin work in Lamar.

Jan. 20, 1905: Mr. Long had been scouring the country, looking for suitable timber for railroad ties, the *Optic* reported. "Everyone with timber who wants to sell ties can do so now," the paper said. The railroad would provide broad axes and saws for the work.

Jan. 22, 1905: The first ties for the railroad were delivered to Jerico. The microfilm copy of the *Optic's* melodramatic account the following Friday ranges from difficult to impossible to read.

It begins, "Sunday while the great majority of our citizens were at their places of worship and the ministers of the gospel were … salvation to a perverse generation from the pulpits of our churches..." and goes on to describe how several men were out cutting ties in an attempt to be first to deliver one to the Jefferson City, Jerico and Southwestern.

Two ties were delivered, the *Optic* said.

"Sunday evening in front of the Holman Drug Store lay a tie with the following written in blue pencil: 'Jan. 22, 1905, 3 p.m., first tie delivered to town. J. H. Stratton, C. S. Morris, W.M. Rannais, A. Lewallen, Spike furnished and driven by Geo. Morris.'

"On the other was written 'first tie delivered to right of way, Hughes and Longacre, taken from Joe Maphies' timber Sunday, Jan. 22, 1905.'"

Mr. Long officially accepted the ties the next morning.

Feb. 3, 1905: A big day for railroad developments. First, the *Optic* reported J. A. Ware's construction train - seven carloads of equipment - had arrived in Lamar. Second, *the Kansas City Times* reported that a man named Thomas P. McDonough had chartered a new railroad, the Nevada and Springfield, to run the 72 miles between those two cities. Previous iterations of the plan had included Jerico as a point on the route.

Feb. 10, 1905: Jerico's rebuilding got a major boost from James K. Peer, like Mr. Whitsitt one of the original Jerico men. Now 60, Mr. Peer announced he had bought material with which to build a new hardware store on the site of the old and would begin construction as soon as weather permitted. The *Optic* said Peer would "get the ball rolling and the Optic looks for a spring and summer of building activity not seen since the first boom on the town."

 The newspaper was right about both the new boom and Mr. Peer, who had dissolved the partnership with his son Preston after the fire the previous June. He not only got the ball rolling but would keep it moving after an arsonist struck the town again six months later.

Feb. 17, 1905: R. C. Laing, a long-time Jerico building contractor, received a letter from Thomas P. McDonough of the Springfield and Nevada saying Jerico would be point on that line. After 22 years of failing to get a railroad, Jerico suddenly seemed on the brink of having two.

March 2, 1905: Mr. Long filed the surveyors' profile of the Jefferson City, Jerico and Southwestern line with the Barton County clerk. It showed the road passing immediately southeast of Jerico, with a station near Anna Edna Cemetery.

March 10, 1905: *The Optic* reported that Mr. Long, in St. Louis, sent Mr. Whitsitt a letter in which he said that Lamar had failed to come up with promised right of way.

The paper said Mr. Long had reported, "that while the refusal of Lamar to get the right of way was giving them a great deal of trouble and causing them much delay, Jerico need not be alarmed or discouraged as they were assured of the road." He said the construction train remained at Lamar, ready to begin work "as soon as right of way was secured sufficient for them to do so."

"Why our sister city Lamar is acting so naughty we are at a loss to know," *Optic* editor A. M. Heifner said.

"The Optic has always held the people of Lamar in high esteem and believed they were men of progress and absolutely truthful in their statements. It now looks to us as if they were extremely selfish and very narrow-minded when they lay down and refuse to act in this matter.

"The very fact that the J.C. J. & S.W. gives them a trunk line and puts them in touch with St Louis direct ought to stimulate every man, woman and child in Lamar to increase that activity. Every enterprise that enters a town adds to its wealth and prosperity ... We would say in all kindness to Lamar, don't be knockers, scrape the moss off your backs and get up and hustle. Kick over a chunk and have something doing," the *Optic* urged.

A more likely culprit than the "people" of Lamar, as Charley Whitsitt surely knew even if the newspaper didn't, would have been managers from the two major railroad systems that intersected there. The Frisco system was the major line out of St. Louis to southwest Missouri and on to the west. It likely had no interest in a new competitor for St. Louis traffic.

Mr. Long planned to connect to the Mo-Pac system west of Lamar but even assuming the Mo-Pac had previously approved the connection, it's possible the managers no longer saw the new route as offering any advantage. Either of the big national roads would easily have possessed enough influence in Lamar to block the right of way transactions needed by the Jefferson City, Jerico and Southwestern.

The same explanation is likely true for the sudden disappearance two years earlier of Golden City's enthusiasm for Mr. McCaull's proposed road.

March 13, 1905: – At a meeting in Nevada with Mr. McDonough of the Nevada and Springfield, the Jerico men offered him right-of-way through Cedar County, depot grounds and reminded him Jerico had a standing offer of a $10,000 bonus ($300,000 in 2021) to the first road to lay track into Jerico.

April 28, 1905: Mr. McDonough, at a meeting in Jerico, dismissed a report in the *Springfield Leader* that his project was "going to pieces," but the paper soon proved right.

May 1, 1905: Mr. Long, in a letter to J. W. Jones of the Jerico railroad committee, said Mr. Ware's construction train was leaving Lamar for a job in Iowa. He said he did not know when he would be in touch again.

Jerico's last, best chance for a railroad disappeared over the northern horizon with Mr. Ware's train. Disappearing with it as well were the plans, hopes and dreams of Daniel Stratton, Charles Whitsitt and Jerico's other founders. The town's path to today's sleeping backwater was firmly set.

21. A revival before the fall

Some of the Jerico men recognized that the failure of the Jefferson City, Jerico and Southwestern was not just one more railroad plan gone sour, but something far more ominous for the town. Certainly J. B. Carrico and Charley Whitsitt did.

For the vast majority of townspeople, though, it was not at all obvious that Jerico's slide into irrelevance was underway. Indeed, just the opposite seemed true. Headline after headline in the *Optic* chronicled the rebuilding of Jerico, with the remnants of the original Jerico men leading the way.

James K. Peer, as promised, began rebuilding his hardware store when the 1905 construction season started. In June, Charley Whitsitt announced the Bank of Jerico's building plans. Rather than build new, he said, the bank would buy J. B. Carrico's Little Acorn Department Store and remodel it. Originally built by James A. Cogle, the two-story brick building at the northeast corner of Main and Broadway had been Jerico's first store.

Mr. Carrico, the story said, intended to tear down an abandoned building north of the Little Acorn and build a first-class business building, a large, two-story brick structure. The demolition was under way within a week.

On July 7, 1905, disaster again. Another fire, apparently arson, destroyed Holman's Drug Store at the southeast corner of Main and Broadway, which had been repaired after substantial damage in the 1904 fire. The blaze also inflicted considerable damage to Mr. Peer's new building, now nearing completion immediately south of the Holman store and sharing a wall with it. Only the "heroic efforts of the firefighters" saved it, the *Optic* said. Those efforts also prevented the fire from spreading east across the alley into the row of business buildings along Broadway.

Mr. Holman said he was sure the fire was deliberately set because benches from the Peer work site next door had been stacked against his building to assist someone getting in. He said he said no idea "why anyone would want to burn me out. If I have an enemy in the world I don't know it." The building, co-owned by Mr. Holman and W. R. Lakey, was insured, as was the drug store's contents. The upstairs tenants, Dr. A. T. Holmes and jeweler E. B. Cooper, lost everything but had no insurance.

With its recovery thus challenged, Jerico again found leadership in James K. Peer. The old soldier simply put his head down and resumed work on his fire-damaged building a week later. The stories didn't say whether he had insurance, but it seems likely that he did. The drug store wasn't rebuilt and the lot stood vacant until 1909.

Jerico, though, was booming again. In July, W. T. Hicks announced he would raze his store building and put up a new, up-to-date one, and Dr. Gates reported he would he would build a two-story concrete block building to replace the Gates-Arnold building destroyed in the fire. He said he had purchased a machine to make the blocks and would begin work when it and the concrete arrived. It would be an up-to-date, first class building, he said.

In early August, W. O. Crosslen announced plans to build a new blacksmith and harness shop south of the Pickett property. The *Optic* called young Mr. Crosslen "one of the good men who have faith in Jerico." Mr. Crosslen later told the Optic, "I thought if I put up a nice building it might cause someone else to do the same."

The Optic in August also reported on a tour of the new Peer store and mixed high praise for the store and Mr. Peer, who "in that time when everything was so dark after the (1904) fire had nerve enough to build this fine house. He was the first man to begin the building."

In October, M. P. Bush, operator of the Central Hotel announced plans to build a new hotel. The same issue of the *Optic* reported on Mr.

Heifner's tour of Mr. Carrico's new business building. The editor pronounced it "among the best in the county." Mr. Carrico headed off to St. Louis to personally select the stock for the new store.

By November, 1905, remodeling of the former Little Acorn into the Bank of Jerico's new home was well under way. It was a major rehab with new entrances and the solid brick south wall transformed by large windows on both the first and second floors. The interior was equipped with the latest banking fixtures.

The bank occupied its new home in early January 1906.The *Optic* said Jerico was proud of the new building, the bank and its management. Later in the month, Mr. Bruster moved into new offices in the rear of the bank.

Elsewhere around town in 1906, Claude Davis bought the livery stable at the south end of Main Street and undertook a rehab project; the rebuilding of the Gates Block was completed and the Carender and Gates Drug Store reopened there; and M. P. Bush completed his new 26-room hotel at the northeast corner of Park and Main, where one or another hotel under one or another name had stood since James Peer's United States Hotel went up at Jerico's birth.

Mr. Peer himself retired from his hardware store after it was rebuilt in 1905, leaving it in the hands of two of his sons. In 1908, Peer Brothers bought the last of the vacant Pickett lots to the south and expanded there with farm implement sales.

In 1909, F. M. Davis, a long-time merchant and father of the livery man, purchased the lot at the southeast corner of Main and Broadway left vacant by the Holman fire and built a two-story brick building where he opened a dry goods store.

As the decade ended Jerico's business district had been substantially rebuilt, with new buildings replacing those destroyed in the fires of 1904 and 1905. Additionally, the spanking new Bush Hotel had replaced the ramshackle old Montezuma and J.B. Carrico had torn down an abandoned store building and replaced it with a fine two-story brick one. Other, more minor improvements also were made. That second boom predicted by the Optic in *1905* had indeed occurred.

In December 1909, the *Optic* borrowed an idea from its past and created a special section singing the praises of Jerico and the region, reiterating many of the arguments offered by Theodore Kerr in his 1889 special section laying out Jerico's assets, from the soil through the climate to the mineral wealth and people. There was one significant difference: The 1909 version mentioned railroads only in passing, discussing instead the "good wagon roads" and ongoing work on roads and bridges.

Railroad talk had not died instantly with the collapse of the Jefferson City, Jerico and Southwestern in 1905. A half dozen lines were proposed over the next five years, some of them by familiar promoters like Mr. McCaull, Mr. Long and Mr. McDonough. Jerico's leaders attended meetings and pledged financial support in a couple of cases but none of the projects got past the pie-in-the-sky stage.

There were short flare-ups of railroad talk once or twice in the 'teens, but by 1910, only the terminally optimistic thought there was a railroad in the future. It was time to plan a Jerico without one.

22. Rebuilding Jerico

The rebuilding of Jerico from 1905-1910 included a great deal more than replacing structures destroyed in the 1904-05 fires. Apparently inspired by the bustle created as the fire-destroyed buildings were replaced, other downtown business tore down old buildings and put-up new ones.

Their results were captured in part by a photographer named Suttle who had a studio in Jerico during 1909-10.

The following photos are all his except as noted. Many of these pictures were commissioned by the *Jerico Springs Optic* for its Dec. 17, 1909 issue, which included a special promotional section.

Guests relax on the porch of the Bush Hotel, built in 1906 during Jerico's second boom. It was still standing in 2021.

This picture would have been taken in 1909, the year F. M. Davis built his dry goods store, under construction on the right here. James Cogle's store building, remodeled and owned by the Bank of Jerico, since 1905, is on the left.

This 1909 photo, looking north along Main Street, captured much of newly built downtown Jerico. Everything is new after 1905 except the livery stable, and W. C. Davis had given it a major touch-up when he bought it in 1906. On the right past the livery stable are W. O. Crosslen's blacksmith and harness shop and J. K. Peer's Hardware store. On the left is the Gates Block, built in 1905 by Dr. Lester Gates and the Bush Hotel, built in 1906 by M.P. Bush.

This 1909 photo captures the newly built Davis Dry Goods store, completed that year to replace the Holman Drug Store, which had been heavily damaged in the 1904 fires, repaired and then destroyed by fire in 1905. To its right is J. K. Peer's hardware store, which had been destroyed in the 1904 fire and, as rebuilding neared completion, damaged again in the 1905 fire. Rebuilt again, the store was now operated by his sons.

Jerico's 1905-10 facelift included a major remodeling of this building at the northeast corner of Main and Broadway. Built by James Cogle in 1882, it housed Jerico's first retail outlet, the Bee Hive general merchandise store. Later home to the Little Acorn, Joe Carrico Jr.'s department store, it was sold to the Bank of Jerico in 1905. The major rehab included adding windows along the solid brick south wall, adding corner and side entrances an extensively remodeling the interior. The light-colored building adjacent to the bank was constructed by Mr. Carrico in 1905-06 as the new quarters for the Little Acorn.

The officers and directors of the Bank of Jerico pose inside the newly purchased and remodeled building, which is decorated for the June 9, 1906 Jerico Picnic. Cashier Charley Whitsitt is in the teller's cage. On his right are Lafe Six, unknown, C. W. Brownlee, J. W. Nebelsick, and C. E. Brown. To Mr. Whitsitt's left are his son Ben and attorney Francis. M. Bruster, whose office was in the bank building. Mr. Nebelsick, a hardware dealer and undertaker, was the bank's president. (Photo from Dr. Bill Neale Collection)

The Gates Block in Jerico in 1909...Built in 1906 By Dr. Lester Gates to replace a similar building destroyed in the 1904 fires, the building's tenants included the Woodmen of the World on the second floor. The original building on the site was built by Charley Whitsitt and Joseph Morris.

23. Slip-sliding away

Some of the men whose plans centered on a railroad chose to exit the scene.

First to go was Joseph B. Carrico Jr., who had been there from the beginning, the youngest of the original Jerico men. He had grumped to the *Optic* in 1904 that he was tired of spending money on railroads and getting nothing in return, and he had given up his plan for the Jerico Mercantile Company, conceived with Preston Peer in 1903, to placate fellow merchants. The failure of the Jefferson City, Jerico and Southwestern, in which he had invested much time, effort and at least some money, was the last straw.

First, though, he did his part in rebuilding after the fire though his property hadn't been damaged. He added a modern two-story brick store building on Main Street to the town's inventory in 1905. But in 1906 he made an exploratory trip to California that led to the purchase of a partnership in a business in Downey, Calif., run by Alonzo Hall, another Benton Township native. He sold his new store to J. P. Long, a Jerico merchant looking to grow, and moved to California.

He did move back to Jerico, in late 1909, and maintained a home there for most of the teens though he played no public role. His name appeared in the Optic fewer than a half dozen times during that span. He spent considerable time on business interests in Texas, where Charley Whitsitt visited in 1913 when he and Laura spent several weeks there. Mr. Whitsitt said in a letter to the Optic they had spent a time with Mr. and Mrs. Carrico in Houston, and that the two couples traveled to Galveston together.

He moved in 1919 to Chelsea, Okla., a state in which he had explored for opportunity several times a quarter century earlier. He died Feb. 3, 1927, age 70, and is buried in Anna Edna Cemetery in Jerico.

Francis M. Bruster, most prominent of Jerico's second generation leaders, went next, in July 1909. He sold out in Jerico and after an exploratory trip on which Mr. Carrico accompanied him, he settled in Pahuska, Okla., where the oil boom on the Osage reservation was under way.

Francis M. Bruster and his wife, Millie, in the rear seat of their car, parked in the yard of their home on Mill Street in Jerico. The car, a 1908 International, was the first owned by anyone in Cedar County.

His departure was a blow to Jerico at many levels. A bull-necked man of forward-looking views, he and his family departed town in his 1908 International Harvester automobile, the first car owned by anyone in Cedar County. His law library was said to be the finest in the region, he was a gifted and practiced speaker and he and his wife, Millie, were both accomplished musicians and stars of the Jerico social scene.

The Brusters didn't stay long in Oklahoma. On March 31, 1911, the Optic reported they were in Los Angeles, where Mr. Bruster was "associated with a number of leading businessmen in the organization of a million-dollar insurance company the express purpose of which is to insure bank deposits."

He practiced law in Los Angeles for many years and died there Aug. 3, 1940, age 75. He is buried in Forest Lawn Memorial Park in Glendale.

Mr. Bruster actually was the second of the new generation leaders Jerico lost. First had been Dr. Lester Gates, killed in a buggy accident the year before, on Aug. 4, 1908.

Just 40 years old at the time of his death, the Warrensburg, Mo., native had settled in Jerico after completing medical school in 1894. He was as widely known as a businessman as a doctor — his enterprises included the Gates Block in Jerico, which he bought in 1903 and rebuilt after the 1904 fire, and he was a stockholder in the Bank of Jerico. He was frequently in neighboring towns on both personal and Jerico business.

It was medical business to which he was tending the night of his death. He and his hired driver were returning to Jerico about 2 a.m. from an emergency visit to a farm home when cattle along the road spooked the horses. Unable to stop the galloping team as the buggy careened down a steep and rocky hill, the two leaped out. When the horses and the empty buggy showed up in Jerico at daylight, the quickly organized search party soon found the two. Dr. Gates was dead, the driver seriously injured but alive. He recovered.

James Peer retired from his hardware business later in 1906, but stirred the town up again in March of 1909 when he joined a group of businessmen creating the Farmers State Bank of Jerico to compete with Charley Whitsitt's Bank of Jerico. He was the new bank's president until he died Nov. 4, 1910 at age 65. The *Optic*, in a long and adulatory obituary, said "he had borne adversity bravely and enjoyed prosperity quietly."

He was buried in Brasher Cemetery northwest of Jerico. There's a touch of gentle irony in the fact his grave is near that of Crafton

Beydler, in whose attic Mr. Peer had spent his first night in Benton Township 42 years before. Mr. Beydler had died four months earlier, a major Benton Township landholder at the time of his death and one of the many early settlers turned by the years and hard work into the prosperous farmers who sustained Jerico.

E. R. Hightower departed in May of 1913, though he continued to do some business in Jerico from his new office in Lockwood. He remained in business there until his death Jan. 15, 1923, at age 65.

Charley Whitsitt remained at work as the others slipped away and retired, but he was looking, exploring real estate opportunities in Oklahoma, Texas and Colorado. On one trip to Colorado, in 1909, he and C. S. Brown, a long-time associate in real estate deals, were passengers on a train that collided head on with another. Mr. Brown was among the 10 killed and Mr. Whitsitt among the 50 injured, him severely. His recovery was long and difficult. He didn't make it home for two weeks, with several trips to Kansas City for medical care after that.

He continued a less prominent role in Jerico's business community until The Bank of Jerico failed in the summer of 1916. The reason for the failure is unclear. The bank closed late enough in the week that the Friday *Optic* had no story, and the next week's story was devoted to the successful attempt to sell additional stock in the town's other bank, enabling it to buy the good assets of the Bank of Jerico, thus minimizing the losses there.

Mr. Whitsitt apparently bore no criminal or civil liability for the failure but nevertheless vowed to cover the remaining losses. He turned over all his property to benefit depositors, the *Stockton Journal* reported.

After the bank failed, Mr. Whitsitt moved to Pueblo, Col., where he had visited several times over the years. He was in the real estate business there until his death at age 82 during a visit to Nevada, Mo., in 1930. He is buried in Pueblo. The *Optic* didn't bother to run an obituary.

So disappeared the last of the original Jerico men, the one who had tried longest and hardest to turn the Mystic City into something more than an ethereal vision floating on the horizon

Afterword

As 1910 arrived, Jerico and its shiny new downtown set off on the path time, tide and the railroad gods had decreed. The town still played bigger than it was – nearly 30 businesses and a dozen professional people were available but the Census that year pointed the way it was to go – the population had fallen another 10 percent in the '00s, to 395. It fell an additional 33 percent during the teens, to 262 in 1920.

Farm income and land prices both plummeted in the early '20s, cutting the numbers and spending power of the farmers upon whom Jerico depended. Fires in 1924 and 1927 destroyed four major buildings. They weren't replaced. The last bank failed in 1929. Then the Great Depression came along. More retailers failed. No one replaced them. The Optic folded in 1937. No replacement. There were more fires; there was no repairing or replacing.

The development of the automobile brought no easing of Jerico's isolation. The town had no more luck getting a good highway out of the state of Missouri than it had getting a railroad out of the robber barons at the turn of the century. Indeed, it was the mid-1950s before a paved road reached Jerico. By that time, it had long ceased to play bigger than it was – it played for exactly what it was: A used-to-be backwater where most of several generations found that paved road best used for leaving.

They've left little behind, except a story with a sad ending.

Obituaries

Six of the eight men who played key roles in founding and building Jerico had been neighboring farmers for years. The two men who turned them into town builders, Dan Stratton and Charley Whitsitt, were newcomers.

The division remained in death. Mr. Stratton and Mr. Whitsitt each eventually moved to Colorado and are buried there. Five of the six others – both Carricos, Dr. Brasher, James Cogle and Morris Mitchell - are buried in Jerico's Anna Edna Cemetery, which occupies ground Charley Whitsitt donated and named for his first wife, Annie, when she died in 1887. The sixth, James Peer, is buried in Brasher Cemetery, about two miles to the northwest.

Like so much else about the lives and work of Jerico's founders, their surviving obituaries are most often sketchy or, in the case or Charles Whitsitt, went unwritten. What is available follows, with the obituaries supplemented in three cases by feature stories that add background and personality. They are arranged in order of death.

Morris W. Mitchell, - July 1, 1821 (Blount County, Tenn.) - June 17, 1893 (Jerico Springs, Mo.)

From the Stockton Journal, July 10, 1890, reprinted from the July 4 *Jerico Optic*

A Pleasant Re-Union

Tuesday, Uncle Morris Mitchell reached the 69th mile post of his journey to the land of the Leal. There could be a whole volume written about the life and past history of Uncle Morris, and had we the space we would take up the thread of his life, and weave a garment of facts that would read more like fiction than a true statement. But space forbids, suffice it to say that his family consisting of four children, James Mitchell, of Stockton, William Mitchell, Mrs. Frank Brasher, and Mrs. J. P. Brasher, and their children, gathered at his home to celebrate the occasion. B. L. Brasher, R. D. Shumate, Alonzo Hall and their families, Mrs. Mattie Stephens and her

mother, and Aunt Caroline Clark were invited guests.

Mr. Mitchell was born in Blunt County, Tenn., in 1821. He came to Polk county, Mo., in 1839, and resided in Polk, Dade and Cedar for 63 years. He went with the stampede to California in 1850 but soon returned. He was married in Dade county, and set up housekeeping in Cedar. When the distant mutterings of discontent gathered like a midnight pall over our own fair land, and the black midnight cloud burst its fury on the people in a declaration of war, he joined the fortunes and misfortunes of the land of his birth, and fought as only an American can fight, for the cause he deemed was right, being among the last troops of the Confederacy to surrender.

After this he returned to find his home destroyed, his farm grown up in weeds, and his fortunes shattered. But like all true men he submitted to the inevitable, threw off the sword, and took up the plow, shear and pruning hook, and retrieved his fortune, and to-day he can quietly sit under his own vine and fig tree, and listen to the gentle murmurs of the stream of time, as they carry him to that haven of repose, where we are all tending, beloved by all his children and the entire community in which he lives. He received some very fine presents from his children and friends, and we hope, with those that were at his home last Tuesday, that many more happy occasions like this may come and go to brighten the hearts of his friends before the Master calls him home.

The Kansas City Star, June 26, 1893

Morris W. Mitchell of Benton Township, Cedar County, who was buried on the 18th inst., served in the Mexican war and as captain for 3 years in the 11th Missouri Confederate regiment, Carson's Brigade, and participated in all of the principal battles west of the Mississippi River.

The Nevada Noticer, June 29, 1893

Morris Mitchell, of Jerico, among Cedar County's oldest and most widely known citizens, died Saturday, June, 17. He was about 72 years old and highly esteemed by all who knew him.

Joseph B. Carrico Sr. Nov. 18, 1818 (Nelson County, Ky.) – Aug. 6, 1898 (Jerico Springs, Mo.)

The Jerico Items column in the Cedar County Republican Aug, 11, 1898 contained two reports, one saying Mr. Carrico was near death, and the second reporting he had died.

The old gentleman, Father Carrico, still clings to life, though very frail. His large frame speaks in silence of great strength in past years. Friends, far and near, to whom he has freely mentioned, cherish blessed memories of him.

The death of Father Carrico occurred on last Saturday at 2 p. m., in his 79th year. Funeral services were held in the Christian church, of which he was a member, at 4 p. m., Sunday, by Revs. Jarnot, Greene and Collins. The appearance of a storm so interfered as to cause a confused dismissal - part of the audience hastening home and remaining until the approach of night, when friends carried the body to its last resting place, while the family and friends were for the most part taken home in covered carriages. The grandson, Preston Peer, from Springfield, and granddaughter, Clyde (sic) Walton, from the Territory, came home to attend the funeral. Thanks unto God for his long life of usefulness and good influence.

From the *Cedar County Republican Aug, 11, 1898*

Joseph B. Carrico Dead.

Joseph B. Carrico, Sr., notice of whose death appears in our Jerico correspondence, was one of the pioneers of the county. He came to this county from Kentucky, and has long been one of the best known of the old settlers. He was genial, jovial, and but few men had keener sense of wit and humor. He was always ready with something to provoke a smile without a sting. As a public speaker he was ready and argumentative, springing quaint and effective illustrations. No man who knew him can say that Mr. Carrico was not a neighbor in all that the Great Teacher taught that the word meant.

Had Mr. Carrico received a thorough collegiate education, some of his marked, attractive and distinctive individuality might have been suppressed, but it would not have made him a better man. Always hospitable at home, he was a welcome guest in every house in the wide circle of his acquaintance. This brief notice does not do his memory justice. He will be remembered kindly and lovingly by all, a monument that can only be earned in life-work.

Dr. Joseph P. Brasher – May 6, 1850 (Christian County, Ky.) – Sept. 2, 1899 (Jerico Springs, Mo.)

From the *El Dorado Springs Sun,* Sept, 7, 1899

DEATH OF DR. J. P. BRASHER

Discovered in a Dying Condition at the Roadside Last Saturday Morning.

Dr. J. P. Brasher, a prominent physician and an old citizen of Jerico, died last Saturday night under circumstances that beget a suspicion of suicide. He was called out to see a patient on Friday evening,

and on his return home that night he stopped at a house and called for a cup of coffee. He complained of being sick and took a dose of medicine while there, supposed to be morphine, He then resumed his journey toward home but only went a short distance until he alighted and tied his horse reins to a sapling, and then taking the cushion of his carriage for a pillow he laid down by the roadside and covered himself with the lap robe. He was found there the next morning breathing heavily and all efforts to arouse him proved of no avail. He continued in a comatose condition and death came to his relief Saturday night. Dr. Brasher was chairman of the Democratic county convention held at Stockton in 1898, and was also a delegate to the senatorial convention that convened in this place last August.

He was an able physician and stood high in the steam of the people in the community in which he resided.

From the Jerico Jottings column in the *Cedar County Republican,* Sept. 7, 1899

Saturday and Sunday last were days of mourning for all Jerico and vicinity. It was the death and burial of Dr. J. P. Brasher. Friday morning, he left town, to all appearances as well as ever, and not returning that night was found the next morning between 9 and 10 o'clock by his adopted son. Allie, 31/2 miles west of town, lying on his buggy blanket and cushion. He was brought to town unconscious and remained so almost all the time till his death. Only a few times of a few moments' duration could he be roused sufficient to recognize anything. Drs. Gates, Stratton and Davis worked with him all day but to no avail; death came about 7 o'clock Saturday evening. The funeral services were held Sunday at 2 p m in the M. E. Church, conducted by Rev. DeJarnot, pastor of the Christian church of Jerico, and at the cemetery by the Masons and Odd Fellows.

Dr. J. P. Brasher was born 1850; came with his parents to this country in 1857; graduated from the Medical College, of Nashville, Tenn., in 1874 and was married to Miss Laura Mitchell in 1876. He has lived and practiced in this county since his return from school and has been one of the most influential men in Benton township. He always had a pleasant greeting and a friendly word for everyone. Probably no man in this township was more widely known than he. He was a member of the I.O.O.F. of Jerico and had been a Master Mason for many years. He was an active member of the Christian church

Daniel G. Stratton, Feb 16, 1828 (Richland County, Ohio) – (Dec. 20, 1900 Colorado Springs, Col.)

From the Colorado Springs Evening Telegraph Dec 21, 1900,

D. G. Stratton Dead

 D. G. Stratton, aged 71 years, died at his home, 1603 Colorado avenue, this morning after a long illness. The deceased had been suffering from brain trouble for some time. The funeral will be held tomorrow morning at 10 o'clock, probably from Fairley Bros.' undertaking rooms on Pike's Peak Avenue.

James K. Peer – April 29, 1846 (Shenandoah County, Va.) – Nov. 4, 1910 (Kansas City, Mo.)

From the *Jerico Springs Optic*, Nov. 11, 1910

A pioneer laid to rest

The news of the death of J. K. Peer came over the wire Friday as a shock barbed with pain and sorrow. When this paper last came to you, it brought the news that all that medical science could do was being done, in the forlorn hope that he might again be permitted to mingle with us. Today all that was mortal of our friend and townsman is at rest in our silent city.

J. K. Peer was a man of generous impulse and never forgot the hospitable ways of the pioneer. The stranger, even though a beggar, never failed to find food and shelter if he sought it at his hands. He had born adversity bravely and enjoyed prosperity quietly. He had filled the various relations of life, as son, husband, father, brother, friend, and filled them well. Who can do more?

But he has gone! Another name is stricken from the ever-lengthening role of our old settlers, and a sorrowing widow in the sunset of life, and a lonely home, or left to attest how sadly they will miss him. It must be so; these human ties cannot be severed without a pain yet in such a death there really no cause for grief. His life work was done and well done. He had wearied of his struggle for health and strength, with life's duties and tears, where are you suffering and waiting, he lay down to rest.

Tired, yes! So tired dear.

I shall sleep soundly tonight,

With never a dream and never a fear,

To wake in the morning light.

He was a man who united sound sense with strong convictions, and a candid outspoken manner, evidently fitted to mold the rude elements of pioneer society into form and consistency, and aid in raising the high standard citizenship in our young and growing state. How much this community owes him and such as he, it is impossible to estimate, though it would be a grateful task to trace his influence through some of the more direct channels, to hold him up to these degenerate days, and his very character of husband and father of neighbor and friends, to speak of the sons and daughters he has reared perpetuate his name and emulate his virtues. But it comes not in the scope this brief article to do so. Suffice it to say he lived nobly and died peacefully. The stern reaper found him, "as a shock of corn full ripe for the harvest."

Not for him be our tears; let us rather crown his grave with garlands; few of us will live as long or as well, and fewer yet will the Angel of Death greet with such loving touch.

James K. Peer was born in Shenandoah county, old Virginia, April 29th, 1845 and came to Cedar County, Missouri, February 16th, 1868. At the age of 18 years, he enlisted as a volunteer in his father's place, in the Confederate army, serving from 1863 until the close of the war when he worked to assist his father in providing for a large family. His first stopping place in Missouri was at Sedalia. From there, in company with Uncle Jake Beydler, with whom he had come from Virginia, the balance of the journey was made on foot and their next stopping place was the old Beydler farm, just northeast of town. He came here in '68, at a time when this country was undeveloped. He was at the time only 23 years of age but a young man accustomed to hardships with the blood of the pioneers in his veins. His struggle for a place in the business world and his ultimate success need not be told here. His history is so closely interwoven with the history of this portion of the country and with the history of many yet living here, that is well known to all the old settlers.

In the early history of Jerico Springs, just after it's organization, he entered upon his career as a merchant, engaging in the hardware and implement business. He successfully conducted his business until in the fall of 1906 when he retired, succeeded by his sons. A. P. and E. F. Peer, composing what is now known as the firm Peer Brothers. In 1908 he assisted in the organization of the Farmers State Bank and was elected to serve as president, which position he held at the time of his death. In all his business dealings he was always exact, very particular about paying his accounts and he had built up an excellent credit with the leading wholesale houses.

On September 24 1871, he was married to Sarah Carrico and to this union were born eight children, five girls and three boys. Two of the girls dying quite young, proceeded him in death to the Great Beyond. Of the three girls and three boys remaining, all were able to be present at the funeral except two daughters, Mrs. Myrtle Smith and Mrs. Carrie Farmer, both living in Seattle, Washington. Only one sister, Sarah I. Beckley, wife of T. H. Beckley, living near Bronaugh, lives near his home, the balance of his relatives living in various places in the east. In the year 1867, under the gospel preaching of Jacob Kraft, he was converted and baptized in the Shenandoah river, together with 35 other young men. He at that time united with the Church of Christ. His life as a Christian has been full and complete. His untiring efforts and his zeal for the Master's cause were the prime movers in the building of a present Christian Church here. It stands as a silent testimony to his good name. But greater than all, is the monument he has built in the hearts of men, the example he has set for us to follow the influence that lives after him. He has gone but there remains for us the pleasant memories of association, his individuality and the knowledge that with us lies the power to meet him on that Golden shore were partings are unknown.

James A Cogle – Sept. 21, 1834 (Tippecanoe County, Indiana) – Jan 27, 1912 (Jerico Springs, Mo.)

From the *Jerico Springs Optic*, Feb. 2, 1912

James A. Cogle, who built the first business house in Jerico Springs and in the year 1882 opened the first store, died at his home in the south part of town Saturday, Jan. 27, 1912, at the age 77 years 4 months and five days. His death was due to pneumonia fever.

James A. Cogle was born in Lafayette, Ind. In 1861, was married to Matilda Hendrick, in the state of Arkansas. About 37 years ago he moved onto 160 acres of land, just 1 1/2 miles south of here. Prior to this he served a term as county clerk, residing at Stockton. After conducting store here, he was appointed Postmaster. He continued the mercantile business in connection with his duties as postmaster. During the early history of our city, he was a power in politics and was a leader in the Republican party. In his early life he resided with a brother who was a preacher of the United Brethren. Deceased was a member of this sect in his early life, but during his residence here he did not unite with any denomination.

To this union of James A. Cogle and Matilda Hendrick nine children were born, two having passed to the Great Beyond. The remaining children are now here, having been called by the message of death, although some of them did not arrive in time for the funeral. They are as follows; J. C. Cogle, of Cody Bluff Okla.; Geo. E. Cogle, of Joplin; F. A. Cogle, Opolis, Kansas; Nellie Hall, Nevada Mo.; Minnie Cogle, this city; Charley and Guy of Nowata, Okla. Rev. Hartle, pastor of the M. E. church of this city conducted a short funeral service and the remains were laid to rest by members of the G. A. R., of which order deceased was a member. Burial was made Sunday in the city cemetery.

Thus, one by one the old boys who wore the blue and who wore the gray are gradually but certainly stepping out of line in answer to the summons from on high. Soon their faces will be but a memory. Their names may be forgotten but their deeds and the results of their hardships will endure.

J. B Carrico Jr. – Aug. 26, 1856 (Cedar County, Missouri) – Feb. 3, 1927 (Chelsea, Okla.)

The first following story was written for the *Optic* by F.M. Bruster when Mr. Carrico moved to California.

April 20 1906

Departed for California

J. B. Carrico, his estimable wife and little son, Clifford, departed Tuesday morning, the 17th last (month), for Downey, California, where they will make their future home, Mr. Carrico having recently purchased the interest of J. P. West of the firm of Hall and West in the mercantile business at that place.

Joe, as he is familiarly known, is a natural merchant and has had about 20 years' experience in the business, which together with his punctilious honesty, industry and liberality, not only ensures him of friends and success in his new location but also makes him a most desirable citizen in any community. Joe is never too busy or fatigued to go on a mission of humanity, or on an errand which had for its object the upbuilding of our city or community, or in the further chance of any enterprise for the common good.

Joe Carrico was born within one- and one-half miles of Jerico Springs long before there was a Jerico Springs and he has had his residence within the township where said city is located continuously ever since his birth, until his leaving for California. The writer has been well and personally acquainted with Joe and Mrs. Carrico for 36 years I and during all said time they have been the genial wholesome people that makes it a pleasure to meet always contending for the right and condemning the wrong.

While it is sad to lose these good people from our midst yet we are glad to recommend them as being everything to be desired by those who prize their acquaintance, and feel a sense of pride in the fact that our city and community can be represented in the Golden State by such Noble characters. P. H. Bridger and wife, who proceeded these folks to

Downey are deserving and worthy, and are entitled to the confidence and respect of the best people everywhere. One church and various societies will suffer greatly from the loss of these good people in which they stood high and took very active part.

Signed, F. M. Bruster

From the *Jerico Springs Optic,* Feb. 10, 1927

(Though the *Optic* did not credit it, this likely is the obituary that appeared in the newspaper in Chelsea, Okla., where Mr. Carrico was living at the time of his death. It has several basic errors - Author.)

J. B. Carrico

Joseph B. Carrico, son of Joseph B. and Marry (sic) Carrico, was born in Missouri, Aug. 26, 1856. Converted and joined the Methodist Episcopal Church South at the age of 19. Married to Melissa (sic) D. Hall, July 23, 1878, at the home of the bride's father, William Hall, in Cedar County, Mo., by Rev. Hubbard. Mr. Carrico's father was a Baptist minister; came to Indian Territory (sic) in the early days, preaching the gospel of his Christ. Mr. Carrico was true to the faith of his father and was active in the work of the church until his health broke some few years ago.

At Jerico Springs. Mo., he designed the church building and then supervised its construction. He was a 32nd degree Mason. Life membership in Shrine. At time of death, he was the only living charter member of the lodge at Jerico Springs, Mo., and he never moved his membership from his little home Lodge. He was a member of the M. W. A.

Came to Chelsea, Okla., in 1919. Was stricken seriously ill about 8 p. m. Thursday evening, Feb. 3, 1927. Passed away at 10:10 the same evening. Was feeling well and cheerful up to the time he was stricken. Ate a hearty supper about 6 p. m. He is survived by his wife, Mrs. Melissa (sic) Carrico, a daughter, Mrs. Alberta Bridger, of Los Angeles, Calif., and a son, C. B. Carrico of Talala, Okla. Four children are deceased. Funeral services were held at the Methodist Church Sunday at 2:30 conducted by Rev. Tull, after which the remains were laid to rest in the Anna Edna Cemetery. Masons had charge of the services at the grave.

C. E. Whitsitt – March 6, 1848 (Montgomery County, Kentucky) – April 11, 1930 (Nevada, Mo.)

From the *Jerico Springs Optic*, March 8, 1912

In his 64th year

Family of C. E. Whitsitt, gather at his home to celebrate his birthday

Members of the family of C. E. Whitsitt gathered at his home on Broadway in this city Wednesday evening March 6, in honor of his 64th birthday. The evening was a pleasant one and was enjoyed as all such occasions are enjoyed. Only one thing marred the happiness of the occasion and that was the absence of Mrs. Louise McGuire, a daughter, who resides in Cumby, Tex. Ann was, on account of the distance, unable to be present. With that exception all the family were present. Refreshments were served during the evening.

C. E. Whitsitt has been actively identified with the interests of Jerico Springs since the foundation of our city. He aided in plotting the lots, streets, alleys, etc., in the laying out of the town site. He labored at the spring and in setting out the beautiful park trees and in otherwise laboring for the success of our city. And his energies have not ceased for today he is the head or our financial institution and is identified with the Jerico Milling Company thus aiding in the support of our best and most necessary enterprises.

The Optic congratulates Mr. Whitsitt upon having reached his present birthday anniversary with the prospects of having many such occasions to look forward to and we trust that each year will bring him increased happiness and prosperity.

--

If any newspaper ran Mr. Whitsitt's obituary, it does not survive. That the *Optic* didn't take note of his passing is surprising, almost shocking, given the role he had played in the town. The publisher, Ross Heifner,

A. M. Heifner's son, would have been well acquainted with the history so why he chose to ignore the death is a mystery.

What if...

The principal what-if in Jerico's history – the only one really - is: What if there had been a railroad?

The answer depends on when. Before the town would have been best, and that possibility was on the table a decade before Jerico was founded. An 1872 map of existing and proposed rail lines in Missouri shows the Atlantic and Pacific Railroad Co. was planning a road from Jefferson City, Mo. southwest to Baxter Springs, Kan. that passed directly by the future site of Jerico.

Fed by that road, Jerico's initial boom would undoubtedly been have been larger and longer. Easier access would have meant more visitors to the springs, which in turn would have driven greater investments in resort facilities and made Jerico more competitive with El Dorado.

The road also would have made Jerico's merchants more competitive by driving down transportation costs, and would have improved the market reach of area farmers.

The Atlantic and Pacific dropped its plan but the route drew railroad developers for another 40 years. At least three of the plans backed by Jerico over the years connected the Jefferson City area and Oklahoma.

The next critical moment came in the early 1890s when the Lutheran Church backed off a plan to build a large community and college near Jerico because there was no rail service. Many of the colleges the Lutherans launched around the Midwest during the latter half of the 19th Century survive, with student bodies of 1,000-5,000. Such a college could have on its own assured a prosperous future for Jerico.

From that point forward, a railroad most probably would have merely delayed the inevitable. The founders' belief that Jerico could be a mining and manufacturing center crashed against the reality that the area's natural resources fell short of their hopes and expectations. Dan Stratton, Charley Whitsitt and Joe Carrico Jr. engaged in 20-plus year searches for lead, zinc and other minerals besides the plentiful coal. They were among the many Jerico residents in on the search. While they found many veins of lead and zinc, none proved large or rich enough to attract major capital and a railroad.

Index

Bibliography

Campbell's Gazetteer of Missouri, R. A. Campbell, editor, St. Louis, 1874

Healing Waters: Missouri's Historic Mineral Springs and Spas, Loring Bullard, University of Missouri Press, Columbia, 2004

History of Hickory, Polk, Cedar, Dade, and Barton Counties, Missouri, Goodspeed Publishing Co., Chicago 1889

Historical Sketches of Cedar County Missouri, Clayton Abbott, Cedar County *Historical Society, 1968, etc.*

Historical Tours of Cedar County, Mo., Cedar County Historical Society, Vedette Publishing Co., Greenfield, 1977

Lyceum Series: Jerico Springs, Mo., Cedar County Historical Society, Stockton, 1976, etc.

Lyceum Series: Cedar County and the Civil War, Cedar County Historical Society, Stockton, 1976, etc.

Missouri History in Cedar County, Clayton Abbott and Lewis B. Hoff, Vedette Publishing Co., Greenfield, 1971

Missouri State Gazetteer and Business Directory for 1893-94, R. L. Polk Company, 1894

A Report on the Mineral Waters of Missouri, Paul Schweitzer, Missouri State Geological Survey, 1892

The Routledge Historical Atlas of the American Railroads, Stover, John F., Routledge, New York, 1999

The War of the Rebellion: a Compilation of the Official Records of the Union and Confederate Armies, United States War Department, Washington, 1880-1901; digital copy at Cornell University Library.

Notes on sources

Ancestry.com and Newspapers.com were the indispensable tools used in researching this work. Both sites make layer after layer of the past readily available.

In direct quotes from 19th Century newspapers, I've left in place various newspaper style elements of the time that conflict with current rules on capitalization and spelling.

The photos used herein are all in the public domain and widely available, with the exception of some of those in the Dr Bill Neale collection. Those are credited.

About the author

Jerico Springs native John Beydler graduated from high school in 1964 and joined the stream of people using that one paved road to leave town. A job at the *Joplin Globe* the

The author during a 2014 visit to Jerico. (Photo by Mark Ridolfi)

following year led to a 52-year career in journalism, first at the *Globe,* then the *Kankakee (Ill) Daily Journal* and lastly at *The Dispatch* (later *The Dispatch-Argus*), in Moline, Ill. In 45 years there, he did everything from covering government and politics to blogging to running the news staff.

Since retiring in 2017, one of his several pursuits has been an exploration of the origins of the town he left behind.

He lives in Davenport, Iowa. This is his first book.

Made in the USA
Monee, IL
24 August 2021